MARK A. GABRIEL, PhD

A Strang Company

Most STRANG COMMUNICATIONS/CHARISMA HOUSE/FRONTLINE/
SILOAM/REALMS products are available at special quantity discounts
for bulk purchase for sales promotions, premiums, fund-raising,
and educational needs. For details, write Strang Communications/
Charisma House/FrontLine/Siloam/Realms, 600 Rinehart Road,
Lake Mary, Florida 32746, or telephone (407) 333-0600.

CULTURE CLASH by Mark A. Gabriel, PhD
Published by FrontLine
A Strang Company
600 Rinehart Road
Lake Mary, Florida 32746
www.frontlineissues.com

Quotations from the Quran marked SHAKIR are from the electronically scanned versions of M. H. Shakir's English translation of the Holy Quran (Elmhurst, NY: Tahrike Tarsile Quran).

Quotations from the Quran marked PICKTHAL are from the *Holy Quran,* translated by M. M. Pickthal (Asia Book Corporation of America, January 1990).

Cover Design: Justin Evans
Executive Design Director: Bill Johnson

Library of Congress Cataloging in Publication Data:

Gabriel, Mark A.
  Culture clash : Islam's war on America / by Mark A. Gabriel. -- 1st ed.
      p. cm.
  ISBN-13: 978-1-59979-212-5
  1. Islam--Controversial literature. 2. Islam--Doctrines. 3. Islam and politics. 4. Civilization, Islamic. 5. Women in Islam. 6. Women's rights--Religious aspects--Islam. 7. Islamic countries--Relations--United States. 8. United States--Relations--Islamic countries. I. Title.
  BT1170.G324 2007
  297.2'7--dc22

                                        2007021752

First Edition

07 08 09 10 11— 987654321
Printed in the United States of America

I dedicate this book to the United States of America.

*I am so thankful the Lord has brought me to America—
the capital of freedom and security on our planet.
Whatever I do the rest of my life to serve this country,
I will never be able to repay my debt.*

*I am writing this book because I don't want to see any moment
in the future when Americans suffer the way I suffered—
not for committing a crime against anyone but for using my free
will to make a choice about my beliefs. I want Americans to
continue to enjoy freedom of worship, whether that means
reverence for Jesus Christ, Buddha, Yahweh, or any form of God.*

*America, you have taught me that everyone has a basic right to
choose what to believe. I am grateful to enjoy that right today.*

CONTENTS

Preface   vii

Section I: The Foundation of Islamic Culture

1 How Muhammad Created Islamic Culture   1
2 The Past Rules the Present   9

Section II: The Nature of Islamic Culture

3 Prayer and Washing   17
4 Fasting and Pilgrimage   25
5 Daily Life   33
6 Stereotypes About Non-Muslims   43
7 The Wall Between Muslims and Non-Muslims   50
8 Personality Traits That Cripple Muslim Society   61

Section III: Women in Islamic Culture

9 Muhammad's Stereotypes About Women   75
10 Islamic Law About Marriage   86
11 Women's Rights Under Islam   96
12 Loss of Freedom for Women   100

Section IV: The Clash Between Islamic Culture and American Law

13 Seven Ways Islamic Law Clashes With Western Law   111
14 What Islam Teaches About Democracy   139

15 Establishing Democracy in Iraq and the
Middle East   151

16 Separating Religion and Politics   161

Section V: The Future of the Culture Clash

17 Fifty Years From Now   167

18 The War of Ideas   171

Epilogue: Resolving the Culture Clash   176

Notes   178

Glossary   190

Bibliography   194

Index of Quranic References   195

Topical Index   196

Author's Academic Credentials   201

PREFACE

AMERICANS HEAR A LOT OF PEOPLE SAY, "ISLAM TEACHES peace." But Americans aren't stupid. They see what Muslim radicals are doing around the world, and they know that something in the teachings of Islam is what fuels their actions.

My goal in this book is to help the world understand that radical Islam is not just fighting Western foreign policy. It is fighting Western culture because the culture of the West and the culture of Islam *as it was practiced by Muhammad* cannot coexist.

For Americans, this conflict is not a problem. Tolerance seems to be the highest virtue in American society, and Americans believe in the saying "live and let live." But this sentiment has no support in the teachings of Islam.

Part of the battle is fought with guns, tanks, and intelligence. Another part is fought with the printed letters on the page. This is the battle of ideas, and I am in that fight.

Smoke Screen

One of the things that frustrates me the most is hearing somebody from the Middle East declare, "Islam is a religion of peace," because I know that he knows better. That person is deliberately trying to make Islam look better to the Western mind-set. For a while, Americans accepted this smoke screen because it was what they wanted to hear. However, the world is recognizing that there is a difference between "the way things are" and "the way we would like them to be."

For example, Americans would like to believe that radical

Muslims are grossly distorting the legacy of the Quran and Muhammad. But in reality, the radicals are giving the most straightforward presentation of Islam. Americans would like to believe that Islam is characterized by forgiveness and love and that the parts about war are just minor diversions. But in reality, the Quran is full of references to war, and the concepts forgiveness and love are but a minor part.

As someone who grew up in Egypt and lived a devout Muslim life until the age of thirty-six, I am not going to play shadow games with you. By the age of twelve, I had memorized the Quran. Later, I earned a PhD from Al-Azhar University, where I lectured. I was the imam of a mosque. Eventually I chose to reject Islam of my own free will, and as a result I was forced to flee the country to save my life.

You don't have to believe what I'm saying just because I say it. In this book and my other books I give information directly from the Quran and the life of Muhammad (called *hadith*) so that you can see it for yourself and draw your own conclusions. Go ahead and read other books and other sources, and then establish your own informed point of view. Just remember: the way things are may not be the way you would like them to be.

The Difference Between People and Philosophy

When people are exposed to deeper teachings about Islam for the first time, they tend to become angry. The problem occurs when they direct their anger at Muslims when, in fact, their anger should be toward the teachings of Islam.

There can be huge differences between what Islam teaches and what Muslims believe. Do not let anger and frustration about the teachings of Islam be transferred onto the Muslim people. The Muslim people are suffering enough from Islam already.

It helps to divide Muslims into some basic categories according to what they *know* about Islam and what they are willing to put into *practice*. These categories are:

- Liberal
- Ordinary, secular
- Committed
- Radical, fundamentalist

These categories provide a general overview of how an individual in that group behaves. I recognize that there will always be individuals who do not fit neatly into a category. But in order to have any kind of understanding of the Muslim world, you need to recognize these categories exist.

Liberal Muslims

A liberal Muslim is usually a highly educated person, such as an engineer, a doctor, a lawyer, or a journalist. He still professes to be Muslim, but he wants Islam to be modernized. The liberal is willing to speak out against radicals and to support America. He may even promote making peace between Muslim countries and the State of Israel.

Liberal Muslims don't keep the traditions of Islam, such as keeping the Fast of Ramadan or praying five times a day. They dress like Westerners and listen to Western music. They aren't ruled by Islam.

Western Muslims are more likely to fall into this category than those still living in the Muslim world. I would estimate that about 5 percent of Muslims worldwide are liberal.

Ordinary, Secular Muslims

These people are Muslim by culture and tradition more than by personal conviction. The ordinary, secular Muslim often does not have an in-depth understanding of the teachings of Islam. He always has to ask the imam of the mosque questions about the regulations of Islam, such as fasting, prayer, or divorce. The committed Muslim, on the contrary, will know the answer. The ordinary Muslim will know about the ban on adoption or the law of *hijab*, but he won't know the stories about the originations of these laws. (I will tell some of these stories later in the book.)

Even though they don't have a deep understanding of Islam, ordinary Muslims identify strongly with being Muslim. At the same time, they don't want to participate in jihad. They are frustrated with the radicals who attack other Muslims and hurt the reputation of Islam all over the world. They don't believe women need to cover up and stay at home in order to be good Muslims.

The majority of Muslims around the world fall into this category. They may be living in the West and going to liberal mosques where the imam preaches a kind and peaceful Islam that sounds a lot like Christianity, and their knowledge is limited to what the imam tells them. Or they may be living in Muslim countries with secular, liberal governments. Or they may be living in non-Arab Muslim countries where their knowledge about Islam is very limited. They cannot read and understand the Quran for themselves.

Many secular Muslims reexamined their faith after 9/11. They couldn't believe that the Quran could be used to justify those attacks. A good example is the story of author Ayaan Hirsi Ali. Ali is the author of the book *Infidel* and served in the Dutch Parliament before coming to live in the United States. Born in Somalia, she grew up in a Muslim family that forced Islam upon her with beatings and quotes from the life of Muhammad. Yet she did not renounce Islam until after Al-Qaeda's attack on America. She explained:

> The real moment, for me, was after the 11th of September. I started to download bin Laden's propaganda and compare it to what was written in the Qur'an, just to check if it was really there. It was, and I was really disappointed and deeply disturbed.[1]

Many other ordinary Muslims had the same experience after 9/11. They went to the Quran to find out if the radicals were quoting it correctly and were shocked to discover that they were. I believe ordinary Muslims need to look more deeply at the teachings of Islam. They need to see the example that Muhammad set and decide for themselves whether this is the example they want to endorse.

It is not possible to say for certain what percentage of Muslims is ordinary, but my estimation is about 75 percent worldwide. Of course, you will find a higher percentage of ordinary Muslims in the West than in a typical Muslim country like Egypt or a more radical country like Iran. That's because Egypt or similar countries will have a higher percentage of committed Muslims and therefore a lower percentage of ordinary Muslims.

Some people think that Muslims living in the West are significantly different from the ones who are still living in Muslim countries. In my opinion, that's not true. I think the Muslims in the West are not much different from the ones in the Middle East. The ones in the West stay very connected to the Muslim community. They speak Arabic at home and eat the same foods as those in the mother country. Some women wear *hijab* and some men wear long beards. There is no difference between a mosque in the West and a mosque in the Middle East. Muslims may change their address, but they don't change their culture. This is because religion and culture are fused together in their lives.

Committed Muslims

A committed Muslim makes great efforts to live according to Islam. He prays five times a day, gives alms, and fasts during Ramadan. This person probably comes from a Muslim family and lives within a Muslim community or nation. He is reading the Quran and hadith for himself and/or listening to religious leaders who are presenting a complete picture of the Islamic way of life. This type of Muslim is aware of Islamic law about women, apostates, sexual relations, slander, murder, jihad, and so on.

This person lives on the edge of a decision. Though he knows the teachings of Islam and works hard to follow most of them, he is not yet committed to putting all of Islamic law into practice. When I was studying and teaching Islam at Al-Azhar University in Cairo, I would have been in this category. I knew the teachings of the Quran because I had memorized it. I had also memorized portions of the hadith and read all of the important histories of Muhammad. I understood what Muhammad required of the Muslims. But I was not willing to put all of it into practice. I had no desire to see people's hands chopped off for stealing or to see people being killed for leaving Islam.

Neither did most of the people of Egypt, which is why the

Egyptian government was not implementing Islamic law. But if you asked a Muslim on the street if he believed in all of the Quran and the teachings of the prophet Muhammad, he would say yes.

So, this is the picture of committed Muslims—they know and they believe, but they hesitate to enforce all of Islamic law. They are not ready to participate in physical jihad, either.

It is not possible to say for certain what percentage of Muslims is committed, but in Egypt, I estimate that 30 percent are committed Muslims. Egypt would be typical of most Muslim countries in the world. In a radical country like Iran, the number is more like 40 percent. Worldwide, my guess is at least 20 percent of Muslims are committed, and possibly more.

Radical, Fundamentalist Muslims

This is the category of Muslim who *knows, believes,* and *practices* the teachings of Islam. The media would call this person a *radical Muslim* or *radical fundamentalist.* The term *radical* should not be understood in the sense of a "radical departure from the teachings of Muhammad." The word *radical* should be understood as describing the actions these Muslims take.

A radical will want to practice Islamic law—all of it—as I describe it in this book. The radical will also follow Muhammad's example of jihad in order to create a place on Earth where the Islamic way of life can be practiced completely.

The committed Muslim knows that these radicals are living according to the way of life that was established by Muhammad. A committed Muslim will cross the line and become a radical Muslim under different types of pressure. Some recent examples include:

- *American-led invasions of Afghanistan and Iraq.* Muslims perceived the invasions as attacks against Islam as a religion. Committed Muslims will join radical groups to defend Islam against perceived attack.

- *Poor treatment of Muslims by America and the West.* Committed Muslims get angry when they hear reports like those of American soldiers abusing prisoners in Guantanamo Bay and Abu Ghraib, or of CIA kidnappings of terrorist suspects. Even if some of these reports are inflated in the Muslim media, they are still going to motivate the committed Muslim to become radical.

- *Poor treatment of radical and committed Muslims by national governments in the Middle East.* When the committed and radical Muslims are put down by governments in the Middle East, the committed Muslims want to fight back.

- *Westernization and modernization of Muslim countries.* The committed Muslims living in Egypt, Lebanon, or Syria, for example, see their countries being influenced by Western culture. They see women enjoying more freedom and not wearing the *hijab*, which appears very disrespectful to them. To bring back Islamic law and culture, the committed Muslim will fight with the radicals.

- *Muslim writers who criticize Islam.* Committed Muslims do not want to allow liberal Muslims to question anything about the teachings of Islam or their application. When this kind of writing appears in the local paper, books, or other media, the committed Muslim reacts.

- *Having friends die while fighting for Islam.* The committed Muslims will have radical friends who have died fighting for Islam due to persecution from the national government or from fighting in a place like Iraq. The death of friends pushes them to become radical.

The Muslim radical is often stereotyped as a person who is so economically disadvantaged that he seses no hope and is willing to throw his life away to fight against his oppressors. Economy has some effect on pressuring a Muslim to become radical, but it is not the main reason at all. The real reason is religion.

You can recognize a radical by whether or not he takes action to implement Islamic law and jihad. To be a radical Muslim, you need to act on all of what Islam teaches.

The Islamic way of life that Muhammad practiced in the seventh century does not operate well in the twenty-first century at all. That is why the percentage of Muslim radicals is small—maybe just 2 percent of Muslims worldwide. In Muslim countries, the percentage would be higher than in the West. In Iran, I would estimate not less than 10 percent of the population is radical. That's 5 or 6 million people. In Egypt, I would guess that 5 percent of their Muslim population is radical. With 80 million people in Egypt, that is 4 million people.[2]

Where Muslims Live

Muslims make up 20 percent of the total world population. The Muslim World League, which is a federation of Muslim countries, has more than fifty members. These countries are spread around the world—mainly in Africa, Asia, and Europe. Out of these countries, twenty-two speak Arabic. (See map on next page.)

When one country is affected, the rest will be affected. When one country is encouraged, the rest will be encouraged, too. These countries are politically and economically independent, but they are bound together by something stronger—the influence of the religion of Islam. They are bound together in history and feeling and in the way they believe and worship. By the way they react, you think, "I am not dealing with more than fifty countries. They are just the same, like one country." For example, if you travel to one of these countries on Friday, you will see the mosque as the center of society. If you observe the social life and the culture, you will find lots of similarities between these countries.

Why are they so similar? It's because all Muslims base their entire way of life on the same sources—the Quran and the life of Muhammad. So the first step we will take in this book is to see how Muhammad created Islamic culture in seventh-century Arabia. Muhammad was one of the cleverest leaders in human history because he built a culture so strong that it has lasted for fourteen hundred years with very little change.

As one who was immersed in studying Islamic life and culture for ten years at Al-Azhar, I will give you the sources directly from the Quran and the life of Muhammad and guide you through this clash of these cultures as the Islamic world meets West.

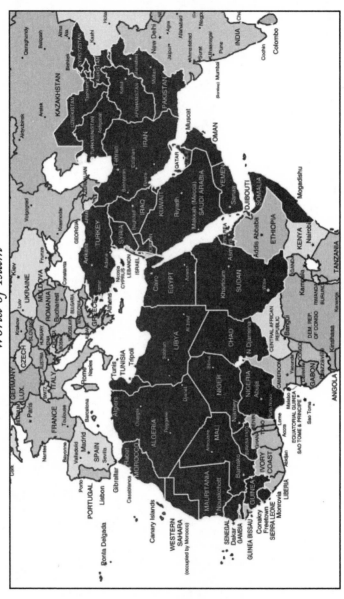

World of Islam

SECTION I

THE FOUNDATION OF ISLAMIC CULTURE

One
HOW MUHAMMAD CREATED ISLAMIC CULTURE

WHAT MAKES ISLAM DIFFERENT THAN ALL THE OTHER major religions of the world? Muhammad turned faith into a culture. In other words, when you look at the Muslim world, you will see that Islam is the culture, and the culture is Islam.

"Wait," you may respond, "there are many differences between the cultures of different Muslim countries." I agree that you can find certain areas of differences. For example, Arab-speaking Muslim countries will understand the practices of Islam more deeply than non-Arab countries because Arabs can read the Quran in the original language. But there is a basic Islamic culture that they all share, and it is based on the system that was established in the time of Muhammad.

The prophet of Islam, Muhammad, was one of the cleverest human beings in human history. He presented a religion mixed with culture to create a way of life. Muslims understand this, and they always say, "Islam is life and religion, religion and life."

The concept transfers directly into politics. Muslims also say without hesitation, "Islam is a religion and a state." In other words, there is no separation of religion and state in the ordinary Muslim mind-set.

In this chapter I will help you to see how Muhammad created this Islamic culture. He established it in such a way that any challenge to the culture is a challenge to the religion itself. Religion and culture are so fused together in the Muslim world that most Muslims can never imagine them being separated.

Islam Is the Culture; the Culture Is Islam

When I was studying for my master's degree in world religion in the United States, I realized that Muhammad did a unique job of taking a belief system and transforming it into a way of life and a culture. He first worked to spread Islam in his hometown (Mecca), and then he went to the neighboring city of Medina, where he was able to establish his military. He took his military all over Arabia, invading and occupying city after city and country after country. This little orphan who grew up in a little, idol-worshiping Bedouin city in the middle of Arabia came up with a way to submit all of Arabia to his will.

Not only that—Muhammad and his successors moved out of Arabia to the east, invading Iraq and Iran, and to the west, invading Syria and Lebanon, and later Turkey. From Turkey, his successors would invade eastern Europe all the way to southern France, where the Islamic military was stopped by the French king. The Islamic army went south and was able to occupy Egypt, and from Egypt they conquered the whole North African region. They were stopped from going further south by the Sahara Desert.

The Islamic military went west from Egypt to Morocco, and from there they tried to enter Europe from the southwest by crossing the Mediterranean Sea and occupying Spain and Portugal. Spain and Portugal were Muslim countries for more than six hundred years.

Muslim traders also went south from Morocco, evangelizing most of West Africa.

In southeast Arabia, the Muslim traders evangelized Yemen and went southwest across the Red Sea into Sudan, Eritrea, Ethiopia, Somalia, Kenya, Zanzibar, and Tanzania.

Muhammad succeeded in establishing Islam because he did

not come with a political system only. Leaders who establish political systems alone eventually fail. They cannot establish a lasting empire. Hitler tried to establish just a political system, Nazism, and he was defeated. The Soviet Union established a system of communism with plans to conquer the whole world. They lasted about eighty years, but they failed.

But the system Muhammad established through Islam has lasted more than fourteen hundred years. People do not know how to deal with this system and this part of the world. Why? Because they fail to understand that Muhammad took his ideas about politics, religion, law, and human relationships and merged them together to create a way of life. Not only that, but Muhammad also declared that this way of life was the way to please Allah and earn paradise.

A Muslim person is indoctrinated and programmed by that system, though he may not realize it. He grows up in that way of life. He cannot think to ask if this is right or wrong. His mind cannot go beyond the line that Muhammad drew.

For example, Islam says that Muslims must fast from food and water between the first and fourth prayers of the day during the month of Ramadan. A Muslim man or woman will never dream of asking, "Why did Allah command us to fast one month a year? What can't it be just one week of fasting—especially if the person lives in a hot place like Africa or Arabia? Why isn't one week enough?"

Islam also says Muslims must repeat *raka'ahs* (the Muslim unit of prayer) five times a day. No Muslim will think to question, "Why did Allah command us to pray five times a day? Why can't it be just three times—one time before the meal—just to remind us to think of Allah and pray to him and give thanks? Maybe three times a day will be fine."

Muslims have no idea what it is to ask questions like that. Muslims don't question the system. It is what it is, and you have to take it. The Quran says:

> And whatsoever the Messenger (Muhammad) gives you, take it, and whatsoever he forbids you, abstain (from it), and fear Allâh. Verily, Allâh is Severe in punishment.
>
> —Surah 59:7, MUHSIN KHAN

> O you who believe! do not put questions about things which if declared to you may trouble you.
>
> —Surah 5:101, SHAKIR

> The answer of the Believers, when summoned to Allah and His Messenger, in order that He may judge between them, is no other than this: they say, "We hear and we obey": it is such as these that will attain felicity.
>
> —Surah 24:51, ALI

Culture Became Religion

Let's look at the process whereby Muhammad established Islamic culture. First, he created a religious system. Then he merged this religious system with parts of Arabian culture, Jewish culture, and some of his own ideas, creating Islamic culture.

Religion is "the service or worship of God or the supernatural." Culture is "social structure, language, law, politics, religion, magic, art, and technology." To put it more succinctly, religion is the relationship between God and man, and culture is the relationship of man to man.

This is why when you look at Islam, you also see the culture of the Muslim people. When you look at the Quran, you will see the culture, not just the religion. When you look at the life of Muslims—the way they do things and say things and act—you will see the Quran. Even if you have never read the Quran, you can see what it *says* by looking at what Muslims *do*. They practice what they preach, if you will.

The Muslim culture is so powerful because Muhammad made the Islamic way of life a part of serving Allah. The cultural requirements of Islam are equal to the religious requirements.

In non-Muslim society, religion is just part of the culture. A Dutch person, for example, could keep all of his Dutch culture but choose to reject Christianity and be an atheist. He is still Dutch. He only changed his religion. But a Muslim person cannot do this. If a Muslim person wants to leave Islam, he leaves behind his culture as well because *his culture is a part of his faith.*

Islam is not merely a religion where you worship God the creator. Islam is your daily life. When you accept Islam, or if you are born into Islam, every aspect of your daily life is controlled by the Islamic system. Choice is minimized. Conformity is maximized. Loyalty to Islam is reinforced from morning to night.

Influences on Islamic Culture

Were all Muhammad's ideas about culture original? No, they were not. He was a Bedouin Arab who was born, grew up, and died in Arabia (which is Saudi Arabia today). Arabia had its own culture, and some of Arabian culture became part of Islam.

For example, Muhammad taught that Muslims should take a pilgrimage (*hajj*) to Mecca once in a lifetime, if possible, and perform certain rituals. This pilgrimage system was already being practiced by idol worshipers in Arabia. Muhammad took some of their rituals (like walking in circles around the Black

Stone) and added his own ideas to them.

Muhammad was also influenced by the Old Testament and merged some of its teachings with his own religious ideas. For example:

- The Old Testament says that the Jews who decided to worship idols and entice others to do the same should be stoned to death (Deut. 13:6–11). The law of apostasy in Islam also demands the death penalty.

- The Old Testament taught Jewish priests to wash their hands and feet with water before entering the tabernacle of God (Exod. 30:17–21). The idol worshipers of Muhammad's day also had a cleansing ceremony before entering Al-Ka'aba. Naturally, Muhammad taught the Muslims to wash before prayer.

- Before Muhammad's time, the people of Arabia avoided eating pork. The Jews also did not eat the meat of pigs because it was considered unclean, nor did they eat meat from dead animals or blood (Deut. 14:8; Lev. 7:24, 26). Muhammad's revelations also forbid Muslims from eating pork, dead meat, and blood.

He hath only forbidden you dead meat, and blood, and the flesh of swine, and that on which any other name hath been invoked besides that of Allah. But if one is forced by necessity, without wilful disobedience, nor transgressing due limits,—then is he guiltless. For Allah is Oft-forgiving, Most Merciful.

—Surah 2:173, ALI

Living Under the System

As I said earlier, I served as an imam in a mosque in Egypt for about five and a half years. One of my main functions was to help the people conform to the Islamic culture. Questions about prayer, washing, fasting, and the like were very important because we were doing these things to please Allah.

It would be common for me to get a question like this. On a Friday morning after first prayer, a man may humbly enter the mosque and approach me with his question.

He would say, "I was with my wife last night, and after that we slept until the next morning. I did not wake up in time to go to the mosque to do the first prayer. When I woke up the sun was shining. Now which type of prayer should I pray?"

Normally for first prayer (*al-sobh*), which is at approximately 4:00 a.m., a Muslim does two *raka'ah* (the Muslim unit of prayer) at the mosque while the imam leads. But before the imam leads the prayer, the Muslim may pray another two *raka'ah*, and that prayer is called *al-fajr* prayer. A whole chapter in the Quran is titled for this prayer (Surah 89). *Al-fajr* is not one of the five duty prayers that must be done. It is sunnah, meaning it is part of the example set by Muhammad.

So the man's question to me was about these two different kinds of prayer: "I didn't wake up early enough to do the prayer on time. Now what should I do? Do I pray *al-fajr* and *al-sobh* now? If I pray them now, will they be accepted by Allah?"

When I answered these questions as an imam, I tried to show mercy to the people and be encouraging. I would say, "Being intimate with your wife last night was not a bad thing. It is fulfilling a duty to be there for your wife. Because you weren't sleeping with a foreign woman or committing adultery, you were doing the right thing. You try your best to obey

Allah in every way, which makes Satan unhappy. Satan made you tired and put you in a deep sleep and caused you to miss that time of the first prayer.

"But when you woke up in the morning, you remembered that you missed a duty, and you were concerned how Allah would view you now. Because the desire of your heart is to please Allah and fix what happened, Allah is very happy. You don't have to pray the *al-fajr* (optional prayer). You only need to pray the two *raka'ahs* for the first prayer of the day, and you can pray them now before the second time of prayer. And you know what? Allah will double the reward of this prayer to you."

This is the kind of detail and concern the people in the Muslim world have for following the regulations of Islamic culture because they want to please Allah. This desire has created a culture where the revelations of the past rule the mind-set of the present.

Two
THE PAST RULES THE PRESENT

W HAT'S DONE IS DONE." "That's water under the bridge." "The past is history."

These are all sayings and ideas that are very commonplace in American society. The past is something that cannot be changed and does not require a specific response in the present. But this kind of thinking is almost nonexistent in the Muslim world.

The Muslim culture is connected very deeply with the past. A Muslim cannot acknowledge the gift of today or tomorrow without connecting today or tomorrow with yesterday—the near yesterday or the far yesterday. He cannot enjoy today without remembering a pleasure from the past. He does not endure sorrow today without remembering some sorrow from the past.

Focusing on the past was part of the culture of Arabia before Muhammad was born or established Islam. Muhammad, however, made it part of the culture of Islam. There is a famous concept in Arabic literature called, in Arabic, "*al-buka ala atlal*," which means "the crying for the past." There is no difference between a radical Muslim or an ordinary Muslim in crying for the good things of the past. They all do it. So now today, wherever Islam is practiced, you will see the past over-shadowing the present.

If you travel to any part of the world and go to a mosque where Muslims say the five daily prayers and sit somewhere inside, you might find the Muslim people sitting in circles talking with each other as they wait for the Friday sermon. They may be discussing religious issues or talking about their own lives.

As they talk, you will hear other people in the middle of the discussion. Although these people are not present in flesh or body in the meeting, they are there in spirit and thought. Though they lived centuries ago, their words and actions still advise Muslims about the problems of today.

When the Muslim imam starts teaching, you will always hear him bring up the past and connect it with today. For sure you will hear the imam or another Muslim say, "What if the prophet Muhammad were living with us today? How would he react to the situation?"

You will see in a very clear way that the past leads, controls, and encourages Muslims to live today or even tomorrow according to the will of Allah and the desire of the heart of Allah's prophet. It would be common for an imam to declare what a person who has been dead for hundreds of years would say about people today. For example, it would be easy for an imam to declare what Umar ibn al-Khattib, the second caliph after Muhammad, would say about American president George W. Bush or British former prime minister Tony Blair.

If you leave the mosque and attend another Islamic event, like a wedding, a funeral, or a social gathering, you will probably see some young Muslim radicals. They may entertain the group by standing up and reciting Islamic poetry. This is an example of what you would hear from them:

We are Muslims.
We are Muslims.
We are Muslims.
We love death and we will never be humiliated.

By the sword,
We humiliate the enemies of Allah.
By the Quran,
We brought light to life.
This is our history.

O people who ask us,
We are Muslims.
We are Muslims.
We are Muslims.

And you will also hear the radicals calling the prophet Muhammad himself, the one who died more than a thousand years ago, to see their position, to strengthen them, and to guide them. You will hear them shouting, "O apostle of Allah, we are the Muslim young. We will never be weak. We agree upon you as our leader. O imam of Allah's apostles, raise up in the midst of us righteous believers. O people, hear our apostle crying and calling: 'Destroy the power of the enemies and spread the word in every valley that we are the soldiers of Allah.'"

And also you will hear them shouting and crying, saying, "In the name of Allah and the name of Islam, we will take revenge and we will walk in our path in confidence to bring victory over all creation or to die in the name of Allah and inherit his eternity. We swear in the name of Allah and in the name of Islam, we will never be weakened, but we will bring the victory to Muslims. We carry the sword to teach the infidel a lesson that he is going to burn in hell."

With these words, the radicals declare their obedience to the past.

Even the media of the Muslim's country—who mostly belong to the government, not to the radicals—know how to do a great business in calling back the past and presenting it in a movie or drama as a nice, delicious meal for the Muslims to watch on national TV or in the movie theater or on the stage. The ordinary Muslim receives most of his entertainment from the state media, which always connects the past with the life of today. He sees shows about Muhammad's life, the lives of some of Muhammad's followers, the Crusades, the Muslim conquests, and other historical stories.

It will help you a lot to keep this simple phrase in mind: It *is* because it *was*. All the major elements that you see in Islamic culture today exist because they existed during the life of Muhammad. It *is* because it *was*.

The Past Sabotages the Future

When you study the history of the early Muslims and you examine present-day Muslims, you will be amazed by the similarity between Muslim culture in the *past* and Muslim culture *today*.

The bond between present and past in the Muslim world has created a great tragedy, especially when the violent past of Islam is revived by radical groups. Because the Islamic world never stops crying for the past, the humanity of the world has been tortured by Islam and through Islam on a daily basis.

The politics of the Muslim world are ruled by the past. Muslims cannot sign an agreement to establish a permanent peace with the Jews because the past says they cannot accept the faith of Judaism. Islam tells them Judaism was canceled by the seal of the prophet Muhammad and the last testament (Surah 3:85). A Muslim also cannot allow a Christian to live next to him as an equal. Why? Because this wasn't allowed in his past.

The Muslim attitude toward Israel and America is especially

corrupted by teachings of the past. There is a powerful belief located deep in the heart of every Muslim that the only reason Judaism and Christianity will ever join together is to bring trouble to Islam and to attempt to destroy Islam.

The cornerstone verse for this attitude is Surah 2:120 (SHAKIR):

> And the Jews will not be pleased with you, nor the Christians until you follow their religion.

The Muslim world looks at America as a religious Christian state, not as the secular nation that it is. And it looks at Israel as a religious Jewish state. So when America supports Israel, Muslims point to this verse in the Quran and say, "Look! The Jews and Christians are coming together, and their purpose is to destroy Islam." The reaction is that Muslims will rise up to defend their religion.

Relying on the past puts Muslims in a position not to trust Judaism or Jewish people, Christianity or Christians. Muslims can't dream of tomorrow becoming a day of peace—a day that every man and woman from every race or religion can gather together as brothers and sisters in humanity and enjoy their lives and help one another.

Muslims have to be delivered from the past so they can see two states living side by side in the Middle East—one for the Jewish people and the other for the Palestinians. They can live in peace, accepting and loving one another. Muslims must stop looking at the Jewish people as the first enemies of Islam, even though the Quran tells them:

> Strongest among men in enmity to the believers wilt thou find the Jews and Pagans.[1]

> —Surah 5:82, ALI

Muslims need to decide that these words from the past about the Jewish people do not apply to the Jewish people today.

Muslims have to be delivered from the past so that they can see the true picture of America. If not, they will keep acting as if America operates according to the Muslim understanding of Christianity—that Christians and Jews want to destroy Islam together. Muslims must accept that America does not equal Christianity. The reality is that America is not solely a nation of Christians. It is a country for all races and all religions, where there is freedom and human rights. No one religion has the power to dominate America. America is full of Christians, full of Muslims, full of Jews, and full of individuals of other different religions. America is not a Christian country trying to lead a new round of Crusades.

The world of today is not the world in which Muhammad founded Islam. Today, the world is like a global village where all people communicate with each other and need to cooperate with each other.

The Culture Muhammad Created

In the chapters that follow, I am going to give you some examples of regulations from the Quran that create the Islamic culture. I will focus on the Quran, not the hadith, because the Quran is considered the highest authority in the Muslim world. It influences the very nature of Islamic culture.

SECTION II

THE NATURE OF
ISLAMIC CULTURE

Three
PRAYER AND WASHING

I ALWAYS SAY THERE IS A HUGE DIFFERENCE BETWEEN LIVING Islam and studying Islam. When you study Islam, you can talk with admiration about the commitment of the Muslim people and how they sacrifice so much for what they believe. You can do all this while you enjoy the freedom of being an unbeliever.

When you live under Islam, the culture is your prison. You are trapped either by the fear of Allah, the fear of your family, the fear of your community, or the laws of your state. Islamic culture invades every inch of your public and private life, from your food to your friendships to the way you wash your face in the morning.

In this section of the book, I want to introduce you to what it's like to live in the Islamic culture. As you read, imagine yourself living this way not just for a week or a year, but for your entire life. You will learn about:

- Prayer and washing
- Fasting and pilgrimage
- Daily life
- Stereotypes about non-Muslims
- The wall between Muslims and non-Muslims
- Personality traits that cripple Muslim society

You will notice one huge topic missing from this section— women—which I will cover in the next section. The status of women in Islam is so hotly debated in the media that I want to devote a special section to give you the original sources of information. I support equal rights for women 100 percent, but I'm not going to debate women's rights. I'm just going to show you what Muhammad said about women and how he treated them. You can draw your own conclusions about how this has affected Islamic society.

For now, let's look at two of the most deeply ingrained parts of Islamic culture—prayers and washing.

Prayer Five Times a Day

Before I left Islam, I would lead the people in prayers in the mosque. This was a very powerful time as our voices joined together as one, reciting the words like the melody of a song. The mosque exploded with a sense of community and connection at these times. Prayer was the cement that bound us together.

Muslims are required by Islamic law to pray at five specific times every day. Prayer means performing the *raka'ah*, which is a memorized prayer with movements. The prayer time will require two to four *raka'ahs*, depending on the time of day, and take fifteen to twenty minutes to perform.

The prayers are the most deeply ingrained part of the Islamic culture because they are repeated every day of the year, five times a day. Prayers are to the Muslim's faith what an umbilical cord is to an unborn child—a lifeline. No more than eight or nine hours will pass in a day without the observant Muslim getting on his knees to affirm his faith.

The regulations and traditions regarding the prayer are extremely detailed. Every bit of them has a basis in the example of Muhammad or his followers. Though Muslims in general follow the same basic pattern, you will see some differences. For example, you can tell the difference between a Sunni or a

Shiite by how he folds his arms during the *raka'ah*.

Muslims must be clean before they pray, and this usually means washing. How you wash and when you wash is a big part of Islamic culture. It becomes a part of who you are.

I remember even after I rejected Islam and spent a whole year away from it, I still washed myself using the Islamic pattern. I wasn't trying to please Allah, but this washing had become a way of life. When I went to take a shower, I would step inside the shower stall but stand outside of the water flow while I did the "minor wash" (which I will describe shortly). Then I would begin to stand under the water coming out of the showerhead, but I was careful to wash my right side first, and then my left. Why? Because there is a hadith about how Muhammad washed himself with a bowl of water and a cup. He would scoop the water out with the cup and wash the right side of his body before washing the left side. So as a committed Muslim, I applied this to my shower. I finally decided that I wanted to kick this habit and keep Islam out of the bathroom. Now I shower however I want.

This is just one example of how the system becomes ingrained in the culture and rules the people. It is a habit you learn when you are seven or eight years old, and it stays with you all of your life.

Minor Wash

Islamic law has a "major wash" (total ablution) and a "minor wash." When you wake up in the morning and prepare to go to the first prayer, you will usually do the minor wash. You can do a minor wash with a bucket of water, standing on the side of a riverbank, or at a bathroom sink. I did the minor wash many times in the Nile River.

There is a specific order in which you wash yourself. First, you take water in your hands and wash your hands three times. Then you wash your mouth, followed by your nose, and then your wrist to your elbow—washing each part three times. You wash your face, and then you wash your ears, three times a certain way. You finish by wiping a wet hand over your hair one time and then washing your feet up to your ankles three times. (See Surah 5:6.)

Now the second time of prayer comes. Do you need to do the minor wash again? Or are you still clean from the wash before the first prayer? It depends on what you did since reciting the first prayer. You don't have to wash again as long as you did not:

- Use the restroom
- Have any discharge from your body (including gas)
- Touch a woman (if you are a man)
- Touch a man other than your husband (if you are a woman)
- Touch urine or feces unless they come from a baby who is still nursing and not eating solid food
- Get licked by a dog (not just touching its fur)

These are just a few examples. The law has many more specific details. Most people end up doing the minor wash before every prayer!

Major Wash

The teachings of Islam reflect an attitude that sex is unclean and unholy. For example, sex is restricted during the holy month of Ramadan because sex is not considered holy. You can see this same attitude in the regulations about the major wash before prayer.

A major wash is required after sexual experiences, such as:

- Having sex with a spouse
- Dreaming about sex and having a discharge from the sexual organs. This applies to men and women, married or unmarried.

There is a difference between these two situations. If a married couple has sex but hasn't done the major wash yet, they can still read or touch the Quran and enter into the mosque. However, before prayer they must do the major wash. But the person who dreams about sex is not allowed to read or touch the Quran or enter the mosque before doing the major wash.

A major wash means doing the minor wash first and then taking a shower or bath. When showering, the Muslim can follow Muhammad's example by washing the right side first and then the left side. But when a person takes a bath or jumps in a river or lake, there are no specific instructions. That's because there were no rivers, lakes, or ponds in Muhammad's area, so he was never completely immersed when he bathed.

The imam of a mosque must understand washing regulations in detail in order to lead the people properly. He sometimes offers teaching sessions between the prayers, especially between the fourth and the fifth prayer (because there is often only one hour between these prayers). The imam can teach on marriage, relationships, fasting, washing, prayers, the life of Muhammad, and so on. Parents may teach the basics of prayer and washing at home, or the kids may learn it at the mosque.

Washing With Dust

The prayer and the washing are duties the Muslim must perform. But obstacles get in the way. Let's imagine a scenario from Muhammad's time about a Muslim couple traveling in Africa. They have had sexual relations, and the time of prayer is coming. Though there is no mosque, they are going to make a clean place and pray. But they don't have enough water to do the wash. What do they do?

Here is the solution: they can use dust. Surah 5:6 (SHAKIR) says:

> And if you are sick or on a journey, or one of you come from the privy, or you have touched the women, and you cannot find water, betake yourselves to pure earth and wipe your faces and your hands therewith, Allah does not desire to put on you any difficulty, but He wishes to purify you and that He may complete His favor on you, so that you may be grateful.

This verse says the couple only needs to do a minor wash with the dust. Even though they would normally be required to do the major wash because of having sex, the minor wash with dust will suffice.

You may wonder, "How do you wash with dust?" I did it when I was in the Egyptian military, and other people did it, too. First, the dust has to be dry. You sit on the ground and put your hand in the dust, and the things that you would do with the water, you do with the dust instead. The exception is you don't have to wash your mouth, nose, or ears with the dust, but the hair you do!

Prayer During Raids and Battles

Just as the washing had to be modified if there was no water, the prayers were also modified for Muslims who were journeying to war. As Muhammad began to send out war parties from Medina, he recognized that doing the prayers could make them dangerously vulnerable. As evidence of the importance of both prayer and war, the Quran gives detailed instructions for praying while on a raid.

First, the Quran says the prayers may be shortened:

> And when you journey in the earth, there is no blame on you if you shorten the prayer, if you fear that those who disbelieve will cause you distress, surely the unbelievers are your open enemy.
>
> —Surah 4:101, Shakir

The next verse says that part of the Muslim military should keep guard while the other part prays. The soldiers are reminded to keep watch over their weapons and luggage so that they will be ready for any surprise attack:

> And when you are among them and keep up the prayer for them, let a party of them stand up with you, and let them take their arms; then when they have prostrated themselves let them go to your rear, and let another party who have not prayed come forward and pray with you, and let them take their precautions and their arms; (for) those who disbelieve desire that you may be careless of your arms and your luggage, so that they may then turn upon you with a sudden united attack.
>
> —Surah 4:102, Shakir

Finally, the Quran says when the military is no longer in danger, they should go back to doing prayers the regular way:

> Then when you have finished the prayer, remember Allah standing and sitting and reclining; but when you are secure (from danger) keep up prayer; surely prayer is a timed ordinance for the believers.
>
> —Surah 4:103, SHAKIR

Conclusion

Prayer and washing are the bones that give structure to the daily life of a committed Muslim. The next two topics—fasting and pilgrimage—are special events for Muslims that occur once a year or once in a lifetime.

Four
FASTING AND PILGRIMAGE

I LIKE TO IMAGINE WHAT IT WAS LIKE IN MUHAMMAD'S TIME when he was establishing the foundations of Islam. As he discusses one of the requirements, like fasting, I can almost see the people crowding around him, asking questions about different situations, like schoolchildren asking questions about an assignment.

"What if I'm sick?"

"What if I'm traveling?"

"What about relations with my wife?"

Muhammad would answer these questions, and as he did, the walls defining Islamic culture became thicker and taller and more detailed.

From this perspective, let's take a look at two of the special duties of Islam—fasting and pilgrimage.

Fasting During Ramadan

Fasting takes place during the Islamic month of Ramadan, which starts at the first visual sighting of the ninth crescent moon, according to the Islamic calendar. Ramadan is holy because it is the month when Muhammad received his first revelation from the angel Gabriel.

During this fast, Muslims do not eat or drink between the first and fourth prayers of the day, a period of time usually lasting from around 4:00 a.m. to 6:00 p.m. Before first prayers, modern Muslims usually eat a light meal and drink a large amount of water, especially if they live in a hot region. After the fourth prayer, they eat a heavier meal and again drink a large amount of liquid.

Fasting of liquids is dangerous for people living in hot places, like the Middle East. I had an uncle who was in his early fifties who was fasting food and water for Ramadan and had to travel to a meeting in another city twenty miles away. He made the journey in a steaming hot car with no air conditioning. When he got back home he complained of a fever, and the family gave him some lemonade and fever pills. However, the next day the fever was worse, and he was delirious. The family took him to the hospital, where he had a stroke and died. The cause was heat stroke and dehydration. My family was shocked that such a thing could happen to someone who was fasting for Ramadan.

Muslims had lots of questions for Muhammad about the fasting. Here is what he told them about missing part of the fast and making up the days:

> O ye who believe! Fasting is prescribed for you, even as it was prescribed for those before you, that ye may ward off (evil); (Fast) a certain number of days; and (for) him who is sick among you, or on a journey, (the same) number of other days; and for those who can afford it there is a ransom: the feeding of a man in need—but whoso doeth good of his own accord, it is better for him: and that ye fast is better for you if ye did but know—The month of Ramadan in which was revealed the Qur'an, a guidance for mankind, and clear proofs of the guidance, and the Criterion (of right and wrong). And whosoever of you is present, let him fast the month, and whosoever

of you is sick or on a journey, (let him fast the same) number of other days.

—Surah 2:183–185, PICKTHAL

In other words, Muhammad said, "OK. If you are sick or traveling, Allah will allow you not to fast on those days as long as you feed one poor person for every day that you are not able to fast. However, even if you feed a poor person, you still owe Allah for that day of fasting, and you need to make it up before the next Ramadan month."

When I was an imam, people would ask me questions like, "I was busy at work, and I forgot that it was Ramadan. I saw water near me, and I took a drink. Did I break the fast?"

I would answer, "No, Allah has mercy. He allowed you to forget so that you could get a drink. Receive that amount of water as a gift from Allah."

Women Missing Fast Days

Women are especially prone to missing fast days. Why? Because they're not permitted to fast (or pray) during their periods because during the time of her menstruation, a woman is considered impure. There's a well-known story about how Muhammad explained this to the Muslim women. He saw a group of women and said, "O women, give to charity because I saw the majority of the people in hell were women."

"Why is that so?" the women asked.

Muhammad explained, "You curse frequently and are ungrateful to your husbands. Plus, you are deficient in intelligence and religion."

"How are we deficient in intelligence and religion?" the women responded.

Muhammad answered, "It takes two women to equal the witness of one man in court. And a woman cannot pray or fast during her period."[1]

Muhammad did show some mercy on women because of their deficit in religion. If a woman cannot fast because of her period, she is not required to feed a poor person. She only needs to make up the fasting days that she missed.

Other Fasts During Ramadan

Fasting during Ramadan is about more than just fasting food and drink. Muslims are to abstain from things that are not holy. If someone insults them, they cannot return an insult back. If someone causes trouble for them, they have to forgive. If someone asks them for help, the Muslims have to help.

Because Ramadan was a time of holiness, Muhammad told Muslims they were not permitted to have sexual relationships with their wives during the time of fasting. Someone must have questioned this regulation, perhaps Muhammad himself. Having married thirteen women during his lifetime, Muhammad clearly enjoyed female company. Ultimately, Surah 2:187 (ALI) was revealed:

> Permitted to you, on the night of the fasts, is the approach to your wives. They are your garments and ye are their garments.

In other words, during the *day* of Ramadan you can't be with your wife, but during the *night* you can. You may be with her from the time of breaking the fast in the evening until the first prayer the next morning. The revelation went on to grant forgiveness to the Muslims who had slept with their wives during Ramadan in the past, before permission had been granted. The Quran says:

> Allah knoweth what ye used to do secretly among your-selves; but He turned to you and forgave you; so now associate with them, and seek what Allah hath ordained for you, and eat and drink, until the white thread of dawn appear to you distinct from its black thread; then complete your fast till the night appears; but do not associate with your wives while ye are in retreat in the mosques. Those are Limits (set by) Allah: Approach not nigh thereto. Thus doth Allah make clear His Signs to men: that they may learn self-restraint.
>
> —Surah 2:187, ALI

There's one last interesting detail about this verse. It mentions that Muslims who are "in retreat in the mosques" may not associate with their wives at all. Some devout Muslims would spend the entire month of Ramadan camped out in the mosque, committing themselves to prayer and reciting the Quran. They hoped to receive a visitation from the Holy Spirit (meaning the angel Gabriel). They were forbidden to have relations with their wives in the mosque.

Pilgrimage

The *hajj*, or pilgrimage, is a perfect example of Muhammad taking established culture, adding to it, and creating a Muslim tradition. Pilgrimage to Mecca is a duty that all Muslims must attempt to fulfill once in a lifetime. (See Surah 2:196; 3:97; 5:97.)

> And proclaim among men the Pilgrimage: they will
> come to you on foot and on every lean camel, coming
> from every remote path.
>
> —Surah 22:27, SHAKIR

Before Muhammad was born, the *hajj*, or pilgrimage, was already practiced. People from tribes all over Arabia would make a pilgrimage to visit Al-Ka'aba, the temple in Mecca, once in their lifetimes or more often if they could afford it.

Mecca was a holy city for Arabs because of their traditions about Abraham, which were also established before Muhammad was born. Arabic tradition said that Abraham moved to Mecca from the area that is now Iraq. In Mecca, Abraham asked Allah, "Where should I build a house for you?" In response, Allah threw a black stone from heaven to earth, which Abraham found and took as a sign from Allah to build the house at that place in Mecca.[2]

Abraham and his son Ishmael built Al-Ka'aba together, and Abraham laid the black stone from Allah as the cornerstone. It was called Al-Ka'aba, meaning "cube," because it was a one-room building shaped like a cube. Abraham's gravesite is just a couple of hundred yards away from Al-Ka'aba. The famous Muslim historian Ibn Kathir wrote that the gravesite was originally attached to Al-Ka'aba, but Umar, the second caliph, noticed that the gravesite made it hard for the people to walk in a circle around the Al-Ka'aba, so he caused the grave to be separated from the building a little way to the east.[3]

Before Islam, the *hajj* ceremony focused on Mecca only. The pilgrims would walk around the black stone set in Al-Ka'aba, kiss the black stone, and visit the gravesite of Abraham. These activities are a big part of the Muslim *hajj* today. However,

Muhammad added a second part and declared that it was no less important than the first part.

He said that pilgrims must also visit Medina. Just as Abraham declared Mecca sacred, Muhammad declared Medina sacred. Muhammad said:

> Ibrahim declared Mecca as sacred and I declare sacred the area between its two stony grounds (lava lands by which he meant Medina).[4]

When the pilgrims came to Medina, Muhammad would lead them in prayer at his mosque. Known as the Mosque of the Prophet, Muhammad built this mosque in Medina, even after he had conquered Mecca. I believe this was a strategic move on his part. He did not want to build his mosque in Mecca where it would be under the shadow of Abraham and Al-Ka'aba. Instead, he built his mosque in a separate city and declared that city sacred.

Muhammad also did not ask to be buried next to Abraham. He wanted to be buried next to his mosque in Medina.

When I participated in the *hajj*, I joined the throngs of people inside the Mosque of the Prophet and performed *raka'ahs* with them. I also went with them to the little building that marked Muhammad's gravesite and peered through the eye-shaped window where I could see a green silk cloth covering the gravesite. I said the traditional greeting to Muhammad: "The peace of Allah be upon you, O our prophet." I also prayed some *raka'ahs*, just as I had done at Abraham's grave.

Muhammad was a very clever leader. He always empha-sized that Allah sent him as the final prophet and the Quran as the final testament. By placing his mosque and his grave in Medina, Muhammad made Medina the second most holy city of Islam and established a place where Muhammad, the final prophet of Allah for the whole world, was the center of attention.

Five
DAILY LIFE

UNLESS YOU HAVE LIVED AS A COMMITTED MUSLIM, IT IS HARD to grasp the concept of how completely the regulations of Islam rule a Muslim's daily life. There are even regulations for how to enter and exit a bathroom! When you enter, you lead with your left foot and say a certain prayer. When you exit, you lead with your right foot and say another prayer. Almost no part of your life is free from the influence of Islam. Muhammad told people how to sleep, how to wake up, and even how to dream.

This chapter will focus on examples of how Islam influences so many parts of a Muslim's culture, including his:

- Calendar
- Prohibited foods
- Drinking alcohol
- Proper greeting
- Charging interest for loans
- Laws for making contracts
- Adoption

Calendar

In Arabia, they had other month names for their calendars, but they were mainly using the Christian calendar. Muhammad came up with a completely new system.

When a Muslim wakes up in the morning, the date on his calendar is determined by Islam. The Islamic calendar starts on the day Muhammad emigrated from Mecca to Medina, so it is called the emigration calendar.

Muhammad established a new calendar based on the cycles of the moon. It is considered a religious duty to follow this calendar because the Quran says:

> They ask thee concerning the New Moons. Say: They are but signs to mark fixed periods of time in (the affairs of) men, and for Pilgrimage.
>
> —Surah 2:189, ALI

Muhammad established new names for the months, including Sha'aban, Ramadan, Dhu al-Hijjah (pilgrimage month), Rabi al-awwal (first spring), and Rabi al-thani (second spring). Those names didn't exist before Muhammad.

Prohibited Foods

When a Muslim goes shopping, there are certain foods he cannot buy, especially pork. But a Muslim is allowed to eat those foods if he is in great need or forced by great necessity:

> He hath only forbidden you dead meat, and blood, and the flesh of swine, and that on which any other name hath been invoked besides that of Allah. But if one is forced by necessity, without willful disobedience, nor transgressing due limits,—then is he guiltless. For Allah is Oft-forgiving Most Merciful.
>
> —Surah 2:173, ALI

Drinking Alcohol

Before the coming of Islam, the people of Arabia loved to drink alcohol. Apparently, some of them were doing their prayers while intoxicated, so Muhammad instructed them not to pray unless they were sober enough to know what they were saying:

> O you who believe! do not go near prayer when you are Intoxicated until you know (well) what you say.
>
> —Surah 4:43, SHAKIR

People who are familiar with Islam may wonder, "Why is this verse talking about Muslims being drunk? Doesn't the Quran forbid Muslims to drink alcohol?" Yes, it does, as the Quran says:

> O ye who believe! Intoxicants and gambling, (dedication of) stones, and (divination by) arrows, are an abomination, of Satan's handwork: eschew such (abomination), that ye may prosper.
>
> —Surah 5:90, ALI

So how can there also be a verse in the Quran that says it is OK to drink as long as you are not intoxicated during prayers? This issue is a perfect illustration of a principle of interpreting the Quran called *nasikh* in Arabic, or *abrogation* in English. Basically, the principle means that in the case of a conflict, a newer revelation cancels out an older revelation. As a result, it becomes important to understand when revelations in the Quran were given, and Islamic scholars have devoted great energy to these determinations.

The verse that warned Muslims not to be drunk while praying was probably revealed around AH 5, while the verse that prohibited all intoxicants was probably revealed around AH 6 or 7. Now understanding these two verses is simple: the newer verse abrogates, or cancels out, the older verse. And to this day, observant Muslims do not use intoxicants, such as alcohol or mind-altering drugs.[1]

The hadith even tells a little story about the Muslim community discovering that wine had been prohibited:

> Anas ibn Malik said, "I was serving wine to Abu Ubayda ibn al-Jarrah and Abu Talha al-Ansari and Umayy ibn Kab. The wine had been prepared from crushed ripe dates and dried dates. Someone came to them and said, 'Wine has been made haram.' Abu Talha ordered me to go and take the jugs and break them. I stood up and went to a mortar of ours and I struck them with the bottom of it until they broke."[2]

Proper Greeting

Muhammad was harassed by idol worshipers, especially during the twelve years he preached Islam in Mecca, his hometown, before he emigrated to Medina. The idol worshipers made fun of him and caused him trouble. Sometimes when the idol worshipers met Muhammad and greeted him, they said to him, "Poison be upon you, Muhammad." It was a greeting of death.

When Muhammad got tired of that, he said, "Allah gave me a revelation of greeting."

> And when you are greeted with a greeting, greet with a better (greeting) than it or return it; surely Allah takes account of all things.
>
> —Surah 4:86, SHAKIR

This verse says to greet with the same greeting or greet with something better. So if someone greeted the Muslim with an insult like, "Poison be upon you," then the Muslim may respond, "The same be upon you." On the other hand, if someone greeted the Muslim by saying, "Peace be upon you," the Muslim may respond with the same greeting or something better.

This is why the official way of greeting used by Muhammad was, "Peace be upon you, and the mercy and the blessing of Allah be upon you." This is the basic greeting—*peace be upon you*—plus something better—*the mercy and blessing of Allah.* This is the complete official greeting. Wherever you go in the Islamic world you will hear this. Sometimes you hear the short greeting, "Peace be upon you." Sometimes you hear the full greeting, "Peace be upon you, and the mercy and blessing of Allah be upon you."

Charging Interest for Loans

The Islamic system covers all the important aspects of how a society operates, including its economic rules. Some of these economic rules appear in the Quran, not the hadith, so they are just as binding as any other part of Islam, such as the prayer or pilgrimage or giving of alms. In particular, the Quran says Allah will not bless usury (charging interest):

> Allah does not bless usury, and He causes charitable deeds to prosper, and Allah does not love any ungrateful sinner.
>
> —Surah 2:276, SHAKIR

If this verse seems to merely discourage usury, the verses that follow make the picture clear:

> O ye who believe! Fear Allah, and give up what remains of your demand for usury, if ye are indeed believers. If ye do it not, Take notice of war from Allah and His Messenger.[3]
>
> —Surah 2:278–279, ALI

Here's the background of this revelation. According to the Islamic scholar Ibn Taymiyyah, the people of Taif had accepted Islam but still practiced usury.[4] Allah warned them to stop the practice and to collect their loans without interest or else Muhammad would declare war on them.

Law for Making Contracts

In addition to prohibiting usury, the Quran has very detailed guidelines about the way in which two parties can create a contract. Look at the kind of detail that is in the Quran about creating a contract:

> O ye who believe! When ye contract a debt for a fixed term, record it in writing. Let a scribe record it in writing between you in (terms of) equity. No scribe should refuse to write as Allah hath taught him, so let him write, and let him who incurreth the debt dictate, and let him observe his duty to Allah his Lord, and diminish naught thereof. But if he who oweth the debt is of low understanding, or weak, or unable himself to dictate, then let the guardian of his interests dictate in (terms of) equity. And call to witness, from among your men, two witnesses. And if two men be not (at hand) then a man and two women, of such as ye approve as witnesses, so that if the one erreth (through forgetfulness) the other will remember. And the witnesses must not refuse when they are summoned. Be not averse to writing down (the contract) whether it be small or great, with (record of) the term thereof. That is more equitable in the sight of Allah and more sure for testimony, and the best way of avoiding doubt between you; save only in the case when

it is actual merchandise which ye transfer among yourselves from hand to hand. In that case it is no sin for you
if ye write it not. And have witnesses when ye sell one to
another, and let no harm be done to scribe or witness.
If ye do (harm to them) lo! it is a sin in you. Observe
your duty to Allah. Allah is teaching you. And Allah is
knower of all things.

—Surah 2:282, PICKTHAL

Muhammad is telling them exactly what they should do or
shouldn't do when a person borrows money. He explained that
the contract must be in writing; it must be dictated by the
debtor, or the debtor's representative; there must be two male
witnesses, or one male and two females; that the term of the
debt must be in the contract; and so on.

He left almost no area in their lives without his regulation.

Adoption

When some Muslim children were orphaned after the American invasion of Afghanistan and Iraq, American adoption
agencies wanted to help these children by placing them in new
homes. However, these adoption agencies were sent away and
not allowed to help any of the children. They were shocked
to learn that Islamic law prohibits adoption. Muslim parents
cannot adopt children, and Muslim children cannot be adopted
by any person.

The ordinary Muslim accepts the ban on adoption because
he will never question any teaching of Islam. Religious leaders
explain to him that the people of Islam are the final chosen
nation, the most superior nation on Earth. Therefore, the
Muslim child has a superior position compared to the rest of

the kids of the world. No authority on Earth can rule the life of a Muslim child other than the Islamic law. Even if his parents die, the Islamic state has the right to look after this child. A Muslim child must never be adopted by anyone—especially by a foreigner from a Christian country.

This explanation may seem satisfactory regarding non-Muslims adopting Muslims, but it doesn't really explain why Muslims themselves are not allowed to adopt. To answer this question, we need to look at Muhammad's life, when the ban on adoption began. Most Muslims have no idea about this part of Islamic history.

Adoption was allowed before Islam. Arabian people had no problem adopting someone's children or letting their children be adopted. Even Muhammad himself had a son by adoption named Zaid ibn Haritha. Zaid was a slave who belonged to one of Muhammad's friends, and this friend gave Zaid as a gift to Muhammad. Muhammad freed him from slavery and adopted him to be his own son. Muhammad needed an adopted son because both of his own sons died while they were young boys. His only surviving children were daughters. Muhammad helped his adopted son to marry a famous lady in his family named Zaineb bint Jahsh.

One day Muhammad went to see his adopted son. Zaid wasn't at home, so Muhammad's daughter-in-law opened the door for him. When she opened the door, Muhammad saw her face. This wasn't the first time Muhammad had seen her, but some historians say that when she opened the door she was not fully covered, and it was the first time for him to see her uncovered and to discover her beauty.

Something touched his heart. Before he asked for her husband, Muhammad said in Arabic, "Praise be to the one who changes hearts." The meaning was that he was amazed God had allowed his heart to be touched that way after discovering her beauty.

Muhammad said to her, "Tell Zaid that I came," and he left. But he left in a troubled position. He started carrying this desire in his heart for his daughter-in-law, and he could not tell anyone about it—not his adopted son, not Zaineb, not his other wives, not anyone else.

Even if Zaineb and his adopted son got a divorce, Muhammad could not marry her because, according to Arabic tradition before Islam, a father could not marry his daughter or daughter-in-law. Then the solution came. Allah sent the angel Gabriel with this revelation:

> Allah hath not assigned unto any man two hearts within his body, nor hath He made your wives whom ye declare (to be your mothers) your mothers, nor hath He made those whom ye claim (to be your sons) your sons. This is but a saying of your mouths. But Allah saith the truth and He showeth the way.
>
> —Surah 33:4, Pickthal

In this verse, Allah tells Muhammad that he doesn't have to hide his feelings. By it, Allah was saying, "You can't live your life with two hearts—a heart with Zaineb as your daughter-in-law and a heart to fall in love with her and be with her as your own." Allah also solved the problem of Muhammad being her father-in-law. He outlawed adoption by saying, "Nor hath He made those whom ye claim (to be your sons) your sons."

When Muhammad came with that solution, it was a shock for the whole community—the Arabs who still worshiped idols, the Jews, the Christians, and even his own followers. It was a shock for everybody. No adoption anymore? What's wrong with Allah?

Adoption had been practiced for centuries. Though the people could not see the motive behind banning adoption, Allah had set the stage to give Muhammad what he wanted.

Zaineb was a clever woman. She knew Muhammad had fallen in love with her, so she started giving her husband a hard time. She figured it out: Muhammad dissolved adoption; Zaid was not his son, and she was not Muhammad's daughter-in-law any longer; Muhammad could marry her.

Ultimately, Zaid divorced his wife, Muhammad proposed to Zaineb, and they were married. So Muhammad married his fifth wife, and adoption was outlawed in the Islamic world.[5]

Conclusion

After reading this, do you think the American system will ever compete with the Islamic way of life? You cannot separate the culture from the religion and the religion from the culture. Muslims have to believe that the Quran is the true word of Allah. Whatever the Quran says will be the rule for their lives—deciding what they can eat, drink, or do. How can you separate this culture from the religion?

Six
STEREOTYPES ABOUT
NON-MUSLIMS

STEREOTYPING IS AN UGLY WORD IN AMERICA. If you accuse an American of stereotyping, he will be deeply offended.

Prejudice is another defamatory word. If you accuse an American of discrimination, his reputation will be seriously damaged.

The word *profiling* also has negative overtones in America. Profiling could be a practical method of identifying a person who may be a threat, but Americans fear this word because it could lead them to cross the line from security into stereotyping.

The Muslim community in the West cries out at any hint that they are the victims of stereotyping, discrimination, or profiling. They say it's unfair and violates their rights.

However, the main way Islamic culture forms opinions about non-Muslims is, ironically, to stereotype them according to the teachings of Islam.

To a Muslim, all persons who reject Islam are *kafir*. The word can be simply translated into English as "unbeliever," but many times it is translated as "infidel," which does a much better job of expressing the baggage that comes with this word in the Muslim culture. The Muslim world in general believes that anyone who is *kafir* is impure and untrustworthy.[1]

If your mind was never corrupted by the teaching of the Quran, you might have the courage to ask the Muslim person, "Why do you judge me this way just because I believe differently than you do? You are not God."

The Muslim will answer in a very humble way, "Oh, I'm sorry that you see it that way. Yes, I agree with you. I am not God, so I cannot be a judge. Allah is the only one who can judge you. I only deliver what Allah said and declare his judgment." The Muslim will be giving you an honest answer because the Quran has told him what to think about unbelievers.

According to Webster's dictionary, a stereotype is "an oversimplified opinion, prejudiced attitude, or uncritical judgment." Let's see what picture the Quran creates of non-Muslims and think about whether this is stereotyping. However, let's stop short of saying that *all* Muslims accept this picture. Although most Muslims accept these stereotypes, I know many thoughtful Muslims who do not. They show courage in going against the generally accepted culture of Islam, and I applaud them.

Common Stereotypes About Non-Muslims

Non-Muslims are impure.

In general, when Muslims look at non-Muslims—whether they are Jews, Christians, Buddhists, Hindus, or anything else—they see them as impure people. The Quran says:

> O ye who believe! Truly the Pagans are unclean [*najasun*]; so let them not, after this year of theirs, approach the Sacred Mosque [in Mecca].
>
> —Surah 9:28, Ali (see also Muhsin Khan)

In the entire Quran, this is the only verse that uses this specific word *najasun* to describe unbelievers, but the idea that unbelievers are impure is completely established in the Muslim culture. Why? Because it is consistent with the overall attitude of the Quran and Muhammad toward unbelievers.

This verse specifically says that non-Muslims must not

approach Al-Ka'aba in Mecca, and to this day the Great Mosque in Mecca, Saudi Arabia, is forbidden to non-Muslims. If you go to Saudi Arabia as a tourist today and you are not a Muslim, you will never see the inside of that place because you are considered impure.

This attitude prevents Muslims from accepting other people as brothers and sisters in humanity. It causes prejudice, discrimination, and separation.

Non-Muslims are inferior to Muslims.

Because the unbelievers are impure, the Muslim feels he is above them. The Quran tells Muslims to view themselves as superior to all other peoples of the world:

> You are the best of the nations raised up for (the benefit of) men; you enjoin what is right and forbid the wrong and believe in Allah; and if the followers of the Book had believed it would have been better for them; of them (some) are believers and most of them are transgressors.
> —Surah 3:110, SHAKIR

This verse tells Muslims they are the best because they have replaced the "followers of the Book." Why did Allah reject the people of the Book (Jews and Christians) and choose the Muslims instead? The Quran explains that the Jews were the chosen people at first:

> O children of Israel! call to mind My favor which I bestowed on you and that I made you excel the nations.
> —Surah 2:47, SHAKIR

However, the Jews were disobedient, so Allah cursed them. (See Surah 5:78.) Muslims believe that all the benefits that God gave the Jews in the past—all the blessings, all the authority—were taken away because of their rebellion until Allah raised the best of nations, which were the Muslims.

Just as Jewish people were considered to be the first to worship the true God and speak for Him to the other nations, Muslims today feel they play the same role. They believe they are the only true believers—pure and sanctified by Allah.

Non-Muslims are not trustworthy.

A Muslim child is influenced and shaped by the Quran from many different sources—his parents, the local radio station, his school, and newspapers. One teaching the child hears early and often is that he cannot trust anyone who is not a Muslim. The Quran says:

> "And believe no one unless he follows your religion."
> Say: "True guidance is the Guidance of Allah.
>
> —Surah 3:73, ALI

Muslims, in general, will be friends with non-Muslims at work or in their neighborhood or somewhere else, but they will never put a high level of trust in the non-Muslims. This is because the Quran warns them against the character of unbelievers in so many places. The Quran says unbelievers desire to corrupt and ruin Muslims and that unbelievers hate Muslims:

> O ye who believe! Take not into your intimacy those outside your ranks: They will not fail to corrupt you. They only desire your ruin: Rank hatred has already appeared from their mouths: What their hearts conceal is far worse. We have made plain to you the Signs, if ye have wisdom.
>
> —Surah 3:118, ALI

Jews and Christians always want to take Muslims away from Islam.

The Quran undermines relationship between Muslims, Jews, and Christians by making Muslims suspicious of the others' motives. The Quran says:

> And the Jews will not be pleased with you, nor the Christians until you follow their religion. Say: Surely Allah's guidance, that is the (true) guidance. And if you follow their desires after the knowledge that has come to you, you shall have no guardian from Allah, nor any helper. Those to whom We have given the Book read it as it ought to be read. These believe in it; and whoever disbelieves in it, these it is that are the losers.
>
> —Surah 2:120–121, SHAKIR

> And they say: Be Jews or Christians, then ye will be rightly guided. Say (unto them, O Muhammad): Nay, but (we follow) the religion of Abraham, the upright, and he was not of the idolaters.
>
> —Surah 2:135, PICKTHAL

So the Muslim is told that a Jew or Christian always has an ulterior motive of leading a Muslim away from his belief. This makes the Muslim very defensive.

The Muslim is also told that being in a relationship with a Jew or Christian makes him "one of them," which would mean that he is rejecting his own faith:

> O ye who believe! take not the Jews and the Christians for your friends and protectors: They are but friends and protectors to each other. And he amongst you that turns

to them (for friendship) *is of them*. Verily Allah guideth not a people unjust.

—Surah 5:51, ALI, emphasis added

Jews are the Muslims' worst enemy.

Usually the Quran speaks of Christians and Jews as one group, but in the following verse the Quran separates them in order to condemn Jews as "the most violent of people in enmity for those who believe." Muslims today still believe that Jews are their worst enemies.

> Certainly you will find the most violent of people in enmity for those who believe (to be) the Jews and those who are polytheists, and you will certainly find the nearest in friendship to those who believe (to be) those who say: We are Christians; this is because there are priests and monks among them and because they do not behave proudly.
>
> —Surah 5:82, SHAKIR

Doesn't this verse help you understand the displeasure Muslims have toward Jews?

Conclusion

I am now prepared to have you say, "You complain about Islam stereotyping unbelievers. But aren't you guilty of stereotyping the Muslim people? You too are making claims about Muslims."

My answer is that I am writing about the Muslim culture as a whole. I recognize that any individual will not match this picture exactly. I believe 100 percent that every individual needs to be evaluated on his personal merits.

However, Muslim culture does not extend the same grace toward evaluating non-Muslims. Muslim culture as a rule projects opinions upon an entire group and does not look to the individual for exceptions.

Seven
THE WALL BETWEEN MUSLIMS AND NON-MUSLIMS

DURING THE FIRST YEARS OF MUHAMMAD'S REVELATION, when he established his community, all his followers were recent converts. The Muslims were a minority in society and sometimes within their own families. They had many questions about how they should behave toward those who had not accepted Islam.

In the previous chapter, we saw how the Quran characterized unbelievers as:

- Impure
- Inferior
- Untrustworthy
- Trying to destroy Islam
- Enemies of Muslims

In light of these characterizations, it is no surprise that Muhammad generally taught Muslims to separate themselves from unbelievers, including their own families.

Islamic culture is designed to protect itself. It creates a system that binds people to Islam and separates them from non-Muslims. The Quran builds a wall between Muslims and non-Muslims that is almost impossible to assault.

This chapter will show what the Quran says about:

- Unbelieving family members
- Unbelieving community members

- Friendship with unbelievers
- Eating with unbelievers
- Marrying unbelievers

How the Quran Erects an Impenetrable Wall

Muslims should separate themselves from unbelieving family members.

Sometimes one family member chose to follow Muhammad while the others continued to practice idol worship, Judaism, or Christianity. These Muslims asked Muhammad, "How do we deal with the family members who do not share the same belief with us?" The Quran says:

> You shall not find a people who believe in Allah and the latter day befriending those who act in opposition to Allah and His Messenger, even though they were their (own) fathers, or their sons, or their brothers, or their kinsfolk. . . . These [the Muslims] are *Allah's party*: now surely the party of Allah are the successful ones.
>
> —Surah 58:22, Shakir, emphasis added

This verse sets up a wall between Muslims and non-Muslim family members. It says, "The believers will not stay in relationship to unbelievers, even if those people were their fathers, sons, brothers, or kinfolk." In other words, your allegiance to Allah means that you must cancel even your relationship with your own family.

The verse ends by explaining that Muslims are part of a new group called Allah's party, which in Arabic is *Hezbollah*. (*Hezbollah* is also the name used by a violent Lebanese radical group that has vowed to wipe Israel off the face of the earth.)

Being in the party of Allah is more important than any other relationship. The Quran says:

> O ye who believe! take not for protectors your fathers and your brothers if they love infidelity above Faith: if any of you do so, they do wrong.
>
> —Surah 9:23, Ali

I had a big surprise when I first came into contact with Western society and Christian communities. I remember how impacted I was when I met a lady who had become a Christian but her husband and children had not. What amazed me was that they were still living together under one roof.

I saw that this wife treated her husband very well, and I asked her to explain how they could stay together. She answered, "My husband and I weren't Christians when we got married, and later the Lord intervened in my life, and he saved me. I pray for my husband and trust the Lord to do the same thing in his life."

When I asked about the kids, she said, "I cannot force my faith on my kids. I will help them, I will talk to them, and I will show them what I have, but I cannot enforce my belief upon them. It is their personal decision. Maybe the time will come when they will acknowledge the truth of God and give their lives to him."

I don't think you can see an attitude like that in the entire Islamic world. If a good Muslim family has a son who is not a good Muslim, they will give him a hard time. You will see a real tension in that family. Why? There is no freedom to have different beliefs. They will look down on the boy and accuse him all the time. Sometimes the boy will leave the family because he cannot cope with the way the family is treating him. (It is usually the men who leave, not the women.)

Even the Muslim community will reject the unbeliever. The pressure is like a solid block against the person who will not submit to Islam.

Muslims should reject any people who are not Muslims.

So the Quran told Muslims to reject family members who did not follow Allah. What about non-family members? Could Muslims establish friendships with Jews, Christians, or idol worshipers? Could they be nice to them? How would they evaluate them?

The answer comes from looking at Allah's position toward unbelievers. The committed Muslim will reject unbelievers because the Quran says Allah rejects unbelievers. Here are some sample verses from the Quran.

- Allah will send Christians to the fire because they are wrongdoers and commit blasphemy.

They do blaspheme who say: "Allah is Christ the son of Mary." But said Christ: "O Children of Israel! worship Allah, my Lord and your Lord." Whoever joins other gods with Allah,- Allah will forbid him the garden, and the Fire will be his abode. There will for the wrong-doers be no one to help. They do blaspheme who say: Allah is one of three in a Trinity: for there is no god except One Allah. If they desist not from their word (of blasphemy), verily a grievous penalty will befall the blasphemers among them.

—Surah 5:72–73, ALI

- Allah cursed the Jews because they disobeyed Allah and persisted in excesses:

Curses were pronounced on those among the Children of Israel who rejected Faith, by the tongue of David and of Jesus the son of Mary: because they disobeyed and persisted in excesses.

—Surah 5:78, ALI

• Unbelievers will lead Muslims to hell:

Unbelievers do (but) beckon you to the Fire. But Allah beckons by His Grace to the Garden (of bliss) and forgiveness, and makes His Signs clear to mankind: That they may celebrate His praise.

—Surah 2:221, ALI

This negative attitude toward non-Muslims colors the Muslim's understanding of the world around him. It affects his personal relationships. It affects his attitude toward a non-Muslim nation. For example, because Muslims consider America to be a "Christian nation," all their prejudices against Christians and non-Muslims are applied to America.

Muslims must not be in partnership with non-Muslims.

During my time as an imam in Egypt, I preached in my mosque most Fridays. I loved to talk about Surah 9:23, which says:

O ye who believe! take not for protectors your fathers and your brothers if they love infidelity above Faith: if any of you do so, they do wrong.

—Surah 9:23, ALI

I encouraged the people to apply the message to their lives. "Don't make friends or do business with the unbelievers," I warned. "The Quran explains very clearly what will happen if you do."

- Allah will not guide those who take unbelievers for friends:

Let not the believers take the unbelievers for friends rather than believers; and whoever does this, he shall have nothing of (the guardianship of) Allah, but you should *guard yourselves against them*, guarding carefully; and Allah makes you cautious of (retribution from) Himself; and to Allah is the eventual coming.

—Surah 3:28, SHAKIR, emphasis added

- If a Muslim befriends unbelievers, he gives Allah proof against himself, i.e., evidence that he deserves to be punished:

O you who believe! do not take the unbelievers for friends rather than the believers; do you desire that you should give to Allah a manifest proof against yourselves?

—Surah 4:144, SHAKIR

- If a Muslim befriends Jews and Christians, the Muslim becomes one of them:

O ye who believe! take not the Jews and the Christians for your friends and protectors: They are but friends and protectors to each other. And he amongst you that turns to them (for friendship) *is of them*. Verily Allah guideth not a people unjust.

—Surah 5:51, ALI, emphasis added

- A Muslim should "fear Allah" and refuse to befriend those who mock Islam:

O ye who believe! take not for friends and protectors those who take your religion for a mockery or sport,- whether

The Wall Between Muslims and Non-Muslims | 55

among those who received the Scripture before you, or among those who reject Faith; but fear ye Allah, if ye have faith (indeed).

—Surah 5:57, ALI

- In the afterlife, Allah's wrath and torment will be on Muslims who take unbelievers as friends:

You see many of them taking the disbelievers as their *Auliyâ* (protectors and helpers). Evil indeed is that which their ownselves have sent forward before them, for that (reason) Allâh's Wrath fell upon them and in torment they will abide.

—Surah 5:80, MUHSIN KHAN

- Only those who are in the party of Allah will succeed (therefore, do not join yourselves with anyone else):

And whoever takes Allah and His messenger and those who believe for a guardian, then surely the party of Allah are they that shall be triumphant.

—Surah 5:56, SHAKIR

Allah promises to punish the Muslim who takes unbelievers as friends or protectors. So what is the motivation behind the Muslims' negative attitude toward unbelievers? It is fear of Allah, because if they disobey him and take unbelievers for friends, Allah will punish them in this life and the life to come.

Muslims should not eat with non-Muslims (except for people of the Book).

Sharing a meal with someone is an important part of establishing a friendship or relationship. It is at a meal where you share not just food but also part of your soul in conversation. It makes sense, then, that Muhammad would prohibit Muslims from sharing a meal with non-Muslims.

I can hear the Muslims coming to Muhammad one day and asking him, "O Muhammad, we are a Muslim community living here in Medina, surrounded by Christians and idol worshipers and Jews, so if one of them invites us to share a meal with them, can we go to their homes and eat their food?"

Muhammad answered them with a verse that says:

> This day are (all) good things made lawful for you. The food of those who have received the Scripture is lawful for you, and your food is lawful for them.
>
> —Surah 5:5, PICKTHAL

This revelation explained to the Muslims that they could eat with Christians and Jews (they are the "people who have received Scriptures"), but when it came to idol worshipers, the Muslims could not eat their food or share a meal with them.

Even today Muslim people will eat with Christians in the Midwest or share a meal with Jewish people in New York, but they will never eat with a Hindu or Buddhist. Why? Because the Quran says Muslims must not eat with idol worshipers, and Hindus and Buddhists are considered idol worshipers who worship more than one deity.

Muslim men can marry non-Muslims (but Muslim women cannot).

Again, I believe the Muslims asked Muhammad another question about living with non-Muslims: "We are surrounded by these communities who have totally different beliefs than us. What should we do about marrying?" This is the revelation Muhammad gave in response:

> (Lawful unto you in marriage) are (not only) chaste
> women who are believers, but chaste women among the
> People of the Book, revealed before your time...
>
> —Surah 5:5, ALI

In other words, Muslim men were permitted to marry
Muslim women or people of the Book, meaning Jewish and
Christian women. Muslim men were not permitted to marry
the idol worshipers. Even today, Muslim men will marry
Christians and even Jews, but they will not marry Hindus or
Buddhists because they are considered idol worshipers.

> Do not marry unbelieving women (idolaters), until they
> believe: A slave woman who believes is better than an
> unbelieving woman, even though she allures you.
>
> —Surah 2:221, ALI

However, the regulations of marriage for Muslim women
are different. The Quran says Muslim women should not
marry unbelievers (idol worshipers), but the Quran does not
explicitly allow Muslim women to marry Christians or Jews.
The Quran only says:

> Nor marry (your girls) to unbelievers until they believe:
> A man slave who believes is better than an unbeliever,
> even though he allures you.
>
> —Surah 2:221, ALI

This is just one example of the discrimination in the Islamic
system against women. Why did Allah give the man a different
standard than the woman? This is a good question, but a good
Muslim will never think to ask it. You don't ask questions in
Islam; you accept the system as it is and just follow it.

Conclusion

I know that this chapter has painted a very bleak picture of the relationship between Muslims and unbelievers. However, individual Muslims can choose to reject—or at least question—these principles. I have met some of these people personally.

While earning my bachelor's degree at Al-Azhar, almost none of my professors had an open mind. Only my professor of modern Islamic history gave me an example of humility and showed me how an academic person and researcher should think.

One of the classes he taught was about the Ottoman Empire. As a class member, I was required to read a textbook that accused the Western colonial powers of trying to destroy the image of this empire. On my own, I also read another Muslim book about the Ottoman Empire that made the same accusation.

By that time, I was beginning to recognize the tendency in my society to reject any opinion that differed from our own. I wondered whether Europe really had a conspiracy against the image of the Ottoman Empire. One day I challenged this professor and asked, "Why do we always assume a bad attitude with the people we disagree with? Why do we accuse the West of hurting the image of the empire, but we don't do the research to find out the truth of the history for ourselves? We are the Muslims. We were governed by that empire. If this empire did good for us or did bad for us, the story will be passed down from generation to generation and we can find the truth."

Instead of rebuking me for questioning my authorities, this professor at Al-Azhar was pleased by my objection. He praised me in front of the whole class for going beyond the written word of the textbook and thinking about things for myself.

He was a very humble man with a friendly spirit. I always

saw him as a special gift during my academic journey. He was really different from the rest of the professors, even though he had earned his PhD from Al-Azhar. He was very tolerant, but the others were mostly not.

At the same time, I had another professor who earned his PhD from one of the universities in Brussels, Belgium; therefore, I assumed he would be more open-minded. However, this professor learned nothing from Europe and came back more militant and radical than before. He reminded me of the radical Islamic philosopher Sayyid Qutb, who spent more than two years in America learning education methods, but when he returned to Egypt his heart was hardened against the West and he became more militant. Qutb went on to write a book that would be a milestone along the road of modern terrorism.[1]

The bottom line is that any Muslim person could rise above the tendencies of his or her culture, but a tremendous amount of social pressure usually prevents this development.

Eight

PERSONALITY TRAITS THAT CRIPPLE MUSLIM SOCIETY

I GREW UP IN EGYPT AND LIVED IN THE MUSLIM CULTURE until I was thirty-six years old. I love the Muslim people, and I am not trying to make others look down on them. In fact, I acknowledge that the Muslim people have many wonderful personality traits, such as:

- Loyalty
- Strong relationships within a community
- Strong family ties
- Helping those in trouble
- Defending the weak
- Determination/commitment to a cause
- Keeping promises
- Hospitality to visitors
- Generosity
- Respect for the elderly

However, other aspects of the Muslim personality destroy part of the good in a person and inflict damage on other people, too. These characteristics cause Muslims to live in animosity with others and within themselves. These personality traits are crippling Islamic society. People don't like to hear this, but it's true.

The reason I can recognize these crippling personality traits is because I saw them at work in my own life, especially when I was young and did not think critically about what I was taught.

One incident especially stands out in my mind. A man lived in our neighborhood who was an alcoholic but tried to keep his drinking secret. He tried every way not to appear drunk in the street. But the whole neighborhood (about 1,000 families) knew he was an alcoholic. Though he never drank in public, people looked down on him and treated him badly. For example, if he had a daughter, no one would marry his daughter because he was considered to be a bad man.

When I was a young teenager, I saw this guy in the street one evening. He had gotten some alcohol, drank it somewhere, and was now walking home. I saw him kind of dancing, and I could tell he was drunk. Because of the Islamic culture that controlled me, I looked at this man as if he were Satan walking in front of me. To me he was an evil thing.

I couldn't just let him pass by; I had to confront him. First, I stood in front of him to block his way, and then I started to insult him. As I berated him, I scooped up dust from the ground with my hands and threw it in his face and eyes. He was shouting and crying, horrified by what I did. When I finally let him pass, he staggered desperately back to his house to get away from me.

How could I do something like this when I was barely a teenager? It was because the Islamic way of life was controlling me. It became a part of me as I memorized the Quran and as I studied Islam in the school.

Islam taught me, "When you see something bad or evil or defiant to the system you have to attack it." So I did. I can't believe I behaved that way and felt good about it.

I am going to describe four of these negative traits and how they are rooted in the Quran and Islamic history. I know these traits well because they were a good description of me when I was immersed in Islam and the Islamic culture.

I am not writing about these personality traits to hurt the reputation of the Muslim people or to make people hate Muslims. What I am trying to do is explain why an entire society behaves the way that it does and how this affects relationships between individuals and relationships between nations.

Blaming Others

When you see a news reporter on television interviewing a Muslim about what he believes is the reason behind the miserable situation in the Middle East and the bloody conflict that takes innocent lives almost daily in Iraq since the war began in 2003, most often the Muslim will say, "It is because of Israel and America." It's difficult to find a Muslim who will not point his finger at Israel or America. He will never say the fault lies with Saddam Hussein, his criminal Baath Party, or the insurgents that Iran and Syria send into Iraq.

You may try to challenge him by saying, "Isn't the problem that Shia and Sunni are killing each other? What do Israel and America have to do with that?"

He might respond, "It is because of Israel and America, and if there were no Israel or America you would never see Muslims killing each other in Iraq."

If I were next to you during this conversation, maybe I would laugh or maybe I would cry. Maybe I would say to this person, "Have mercy upon yourself. Think about your history. America or Israel was not there in the time of Abu Bakr or the time of Ali or the time of Muawiyya when the Sunni and Shia sects were formed. Muslims have caused their own problems."

The teachings of Islam have created a culture to blame others. All his life, a Muslim is taught that he is the best among all people:

> You are the best of the nations raised up for (the benefit of) men; you enjoin what is right and forbid the wrong and believe in Allah; and if the followers of the Book had believed, it would have been better for them; of them (some) are believers and most of them are transgressors.
> —Surah 3:110, Shakir

This verse says that the Muslim nation is better than followers of the Book, which are the Jews and Christians. From the Muslim point of view, North America, South America, and Europe are full of Christian nations, all of which are inferior to Muslims in the eyes of Allah.

If a person believes God favors his nations above all nations, then he will deny that his people are ever in the wrong. This is a foreign policy nightmare.

By the same token, he will have a hard time accepting that he personally is capable of making mistakes as well. He will struggle with accepting responsibility when things go wrong. A Muslim isn't born with this mind-set; it is established at a young age by religious teaching.

I recently heard about a sign that American president Harry S. Truman had on his desk that read, "The buck stops here." He meant he would take responsibility for the outcome of his actions. This attitude is mostly missing in the mind-set of the typical Muslim.

Muslim society is a victim society. To explain their problems, Muslims say they are being targeted by their enemies or by people who don't like them. These are enemies from the

Muslim point of view. The people in question may not consider themselves to be enemies at all.

Craving Power

The desire for power has deep roots in the Arabian Desert. The government in the Bedouin society revolved around the leader of the tribe, and authority was one of the most important elements in Arabic political and social life before Islam. No democracy was being practiced in Arabia; no election was held in the modern fashion we know. The one with the most power or money—be it a person or tribe—was the one who controlled society.

When Muhammad started preaching his religion, he needed to put those who followed him in a position of power. Muslims needed to see themselves as high above the other groups in society. It was necessary for Muhammad to tell his followers, "You are the best—better than the idol worshipers of Mecca. You are the best—better than the Jewish people who live in Medina. You are the best—better than the Christians who surround us in Arabia, Yemen, Egypt, Syria, or Ethiopia. You are the best." The Muslims accepted this honor as directly from Allah as it states in Surah 3:110: "You are the best of the nations raised up for (the benefit of) men" (SHAKIR). The Arabian need for power established itself in the Islamic culture.

This craving for power and authority is one of the secrets behind the political dictatorships in the Islamic world. It started in the Arabian society that existed before Islam and then became a part of the Islamic way of life.

Muslims have been fighting among themselves for power since the death of Muhammad to this present day. Just hours after Muhammad's death, the first division took place among the Muslims over who would lead the Muslim empire. The

Muslims put that division under control quickly by choosing Abu Bakr to be the first caliph, but when Abu Bakr died after two years, the fighting continued to the second, third, and fourth caliph to reach the most horrible day when Muslims divided into two parties—one party supporting Ali, Muhammad's cousin on his father's side, and the other party supporting Muawiyya. The party supporting Muawiyya became the foundation of the Muslim Sunni sect, which represents almost 85 percent of today's Muslim population. And the party supporting Ali became the foundation of the Shiite sect, which represents most of the remaining 15 percent of the Muslim population.

Islamic history to any person—scholar, half-scholar, or no scholar at all—will show that the love of gaining power, the love of having authority over others, and the love of controlling were the causes of Muslims being divided into the Sunni and Shiite sects. This love of power is responsible for killing not just hundreds of thousands but, I can say with confidence, millions of victims. The desire for control and those who have this desire are behind the establishment of Islamic dictators like Saddam Hussein of Iraq, Gamal Abdel Nasser of Egypt, Hafez al-Assad of Syria, Muammar al-Qaddafi of Libya, and others.

Rigid About Opinions

You have to look hard in the Quran to find verses that encourage people to have a good attitude toward unbelievers. But here are the two examples that are quoted most often:

> And argue not with the People of the Scripture unless it be in (a way) that is better, save with such of them as do wrong; and say: We believe in that which hath been

revealed unto us and revealed unto you; our Allah and your Allah is One, and unto Him we surrender.

—Surah 29:46, PICKTHAL

O people of the Scripture (Jews and Christians): Come to a word that is just between us and you, that we worship none but Allah, and that we associate no partners with Him, and that none of us shall take others as lords besides Allah. Then, if they turn away, say: "Bear witness that we are Muslims."

—Surah 3:64, MUHSIN KHAN

But in fact, when Muslims debate with someone about belief they are very aggressive. They will not give you a chance to describe your belief. They are always attacking. Why does this happen?

I believe it's because the nature of the Islamic religion is intolerant of other opinions as a whole. So even though a few verses describe good dialogue with unbelievers, the weight of the rest of the revelation pushes the Muslim to be intolerant and argumentative. The typical Muslim does not see the validity of others' points of view. And even if this person dialogues, it is only when winning is certain.

When this person has an opinion, no power can change his position. He will live or die with that idea.

For example, a typical Muslim has a horrible attitude toward Jewish people. (See Surah 2:65; 5:60; 7:166.) When you see a Muslim today and ask him about his view of Jewish people, he will say, "They were the enemies of my prophet at the beginning, they are going to be my enemies today, and they will be my enemies until the Resurrection Day because this is what my prophet told me."

New information will not change his mind. Even if a Muslim meets a Jewish person who is friendly and kind and fair to him, his attitude will not change.

Think about where that belief comes from. The Muslim learned it from his father, his grandfather, the Quran, and the example of the prophet Muhammad. He will never accept any argument about it. From the day Muhammad preached his message for the first time to our present time, this idea has been passed down. What power in the world can change it?

Even if you say, "Muhammad died, and he is not here anymore. He is not able to enforce what he believed over the Muslim society," the Muslim will say, "Muhammad died in the flesh, but he never died in spirit. His teaching is alive."

Lacking Mercy

The desert of Arabia is one of the harshest places on Earth. When I was working at the University of Tripoli in Libya, they occasionally sent me to teach at the University of Sub'ha, which is located in a city at the edge of the Sahara Desert. One weekend, one of my students invited me to come to his home to see how his people did their Friday prayers.

This student was a member of the Tuareg people, a Bedouin tribe that has lived for centuries in the Sahara Desert in the area between Libya, Algeria, Mali, and Niger. Going to his city was like walking backward in time until I came to the hometown of Muhammad in the seventh century. These people were living the same way.

The buildings were made of mud, and camels were tied up in the street. To protect themselves from the sun and the blowing sand, the men and women wrapped long scarves around their heads and faces, leaving only a thin slit between the strips of fabric for the eyes. To protect their bodies, they wore billowing robes that left no patch of skin uncovered. In the winter they wore black, and in the summer they wore white.

A harsh environment creates harsh people. The Bedouin tribes that populated Arabia during Muhammad's life were harsh and not easygoing. They spent decades engaged in war and killing each other with a harshness our modern minds cannot handle. When Arabs had a conflict, they showed no mercy.

How could these people find mercy in their hearts when they were always committing murder? Where is the mercy in a father and mother who were so hardened that they could bury their baby daughter alive in the desert sand simply because they feared that she would grow up to shame her family by having sex with someone before she got married? (See Surah 16:58–59.)

Muhammad, the founder of Islam, was a typical example of this type of people. He was born and raised and lived and died in their harsh environment. It would be absolutely normal for Muhammad to have a harsh personality, and no one would have the right to blame him for that.

Allah fit in comfortably with the culture of Arabia, calling for harshness against enemies and loyalty to allies:

> O ye who believe! Fight those of the disbelievers who are near to you, and let them find harshness in you, and know that Allah is with those who keep their duty (unto Him).
> —Surah 9:123, PICKTHAL

> Muhammad is the messenger of Allah. And those with him are hard against the disbelievers and merciful among themselves.
> —Surah 48:29, PICKTHAL

Allah not only commanded Muslims to fight and to kill the infidels, but he also asked them to be "harsh." Muhammad was able to obey this type of teaching and deliver it to his followers because he was living among some of the harshest people known in our history.

This harshness was not limited to Muslims against non-Muslims (or infidels). Muslims practiced harshness against one another. They did not show mercy in the conflicts they had against one another. All I ever saw through my study of Islamic history was that the root of harshness was deep and that the tree of cruelty grew tall.

When we understand the context in which Islam was born, we will not be confused when we see human rights and freedom taken away in this part of the world. It will be no surprise when we see dictators, such as Saddam Hussein, standing in public with very proud, proud voices connecting themselves to the house and the family of the prophet Muhammad. Look at the mass graves that were found after Hussein's fall. And look at the hundreds of thousands who were killed by the hand of this murderer. He proved his connection with the family of Muhammad this way.

Jesus said, "He who lives by the sword will die by the sword." (See Matthew 26:52.) This is the fact in the Muslim world. The sword that strikes the unbeliever strikes down any opposition—including fellow Muslims.

Conclusion

I think the only way to fix some of the problems in Muslim society is to expose them and invite people to think critically about them. That is why I have exposed these crippling attitudes:

- Blaming others
- Craving power
- Rigid about opinions
- Lacking mercy

During the expansion of the Islamic empire, the conquering culture introduced personality traits that were learned and passed down from generation to generation. Muslims need to recognize the negative traits and decide whether they will reject them or allow them to continue.

SECTION III
WOMEN IN
ISLAMIC CULTURE

Nine
MUHAMMAD'S STEREOTYPES ABOUT WOMEN

YOU MAY RECALL AT THE BEGINNING OF THE LAST SECTION I said that I would dedicate one entire section to the topic of women. The media have brought the issue of women's rights in the Middle East to the attention of the entire world. I support equal rights for women 100 percent.

Because I grew up in a society where women were easily abused, I have a deep compassion for the condition of women today, especially in the Muslim world. This section of the book will look in depth at the position Muhammad gave to women in Muslim society. It will also include comments from Muslim scholars through the centuries to show how the seventh-century teaching was applied during Islamic history up to the present time.

In the next four chapters, I will describe:

- Muhammad's stereotypes about women
- Islamic law about marriage
- Rights for women under Islam
- Freedoms women lose under Islam

Pre-Islamic Attitudes

When Muhammad was growing up among the Arabs in Mecca, women suffered a horrible level of discrimination. Even the word for *woman* in Arabic society was a word of shame.

Women were looked upon as something shameful and not good in any way.

The Quran describes how the people treated baby girls before Islam was established:

> And when a daughter is announced to one of them his face becomes black and he is full of wrath. He hides himself from the people because of the evil of that which is announced to him. Shall he keep it with disgrace or bury it (alive) in the dust? Now surely evil is what they judge.
>
> —Surah 16:58–59, SHAKIR

It was bad news to have a daughter instead of a son. It was common for the parents to take the baby girl to the desert outside of Mecca and bury her alive in the sand to kill her. On Judgment Day, the Quran says, the baby girls who were buried will be asked, "For what crime were you killed?" (See Surah 81:8–9.) So the first revelations Muhammad received about women declared war against his own culture for burying the baby girls alive in the sand. He declared that Allah would not allow baby girls to be buried alive in the desert anymore. Based on this, Muslim scholars will say Muhammad was the savior of the Arabian women.

While Muhammad did well to stop the practice of burying baby girls alive, he didn't change the negative attitude in Arab society toward women. He didn't even raise Muslim women to the level of respect that was given to them by the religions around him. For example, he was surrounded by Jewish people. The Jewish people don't treat women as inferior. Mecca also had a population of Christians who were Ebionites. These Christians weren't followers of the Bible like Christians today, but they treated women better than Islam did.

So Muhammad saved the lives of baby girls, but he didn't improve the lives these girls grew up to live. He perpetuated the attitudes of Arabian culture. He continued to practice that man is superior to woman.

Women in Islamic Culture

I can give you a clear picture of how women were treated in Muhammad's day. But in modern Muslim society, you would have to look at each family individually to understand their attitudes toward women. The real position of a woman depends on her family. If she lives with a good family, she will be treated with respect and dignity. In my parents' home in Egypt, my mother and sister were treated with honor. However, if a woman is part of a bad family, she may suffer.

The ordinary Muslim does not have a deep understanding of the teachings of Islam. He may know the Quran says men are superior to women, but he may not know some of the ways Muhammad criticized women. The committed Muslims, however, will be very familiar with the teachings that I am about to present.

Now let's look specifically at some stereotypes Muhammad perpetuated about women.

Allah made men superior to women.

The most famous verse in the entire Quran about the difference between men and women is Surah 4:34 (ALI):

> Men are the protectors and maintainers of women, because Allah has given the one more (strength) than the other, and because they support them from their means.

There are two important points you need to see in this verse:

1. Men are responsible to protect and maintain women.
2. Men receive more strength from Allah than women do.

In the same place that the Quran protects women, it also stereotypes them. It's good that Muhammad told his people to protect women, because they needed protection in that society. But Muhammad didn't change the attitude of that society toward women. He still echoed thethe Arabic understanding that women are inferior.

Ibn Kathir (1302–1373), who lived seven hundred years after Muhammad, is one of the most famous Muslim scholars of all time. In his *Commentary of the Great Quran,* he made the following comments on this verse, making it clear that men are much better than women:

> Allah makes very clear the difference between man and woman and makes man superior and much better than woman. You cannot bring any equality between them because Allah has given man more intelligence and more ability to do things and also man has the ability to work and provide for his woman.[1]

Now let's jump to modern times and see how a moderate Muslim scholar comments about equality between men and women:

> It's not fair to make equality in everything between the one whose attention is all on running to the malls to buy clothes and the latest fashion and her hairstyle. You cannot have equality between a person who knows

nothing but this and the one who carries the responsibility and provides for her and his kids and carries the burden and faces difficulties for her sake.[2]

In modern vernacular, this author is saying the same thing: equality between men and women is not fair to men.

Allah made women inferior in intelligence and religion.

Why is the woman inferior? What strengths was she denied?

We can find out by reading a dialogue that took place between Muhammad and some Muslim women. When I read this story, I am struck by how innocent these women seem to be. He accused them, and they asked him why, because they didn't know the reason behind his accusation.

Muhammad didn't say, "This is my own personal opinion about you." He said, "This is Allah's point of view." He meant, "Allah knows more about the nature of women than you know about yourself. Allah is exposing you and telling the truth about you."

Here's the story:

> Once Allah's Apostle went out to the Musalla (to offer the prayer) o [*sic*] 'Id-al-Adha or Al-Fitr prayer. Then he passed by the women and said, "O women! Give alms, as I have seen that the majority of the dwellers of Hellfire were you (women)."
>
> They asked, "Why is it so, O Allah's Apostle?"
>
> He replied, "You curse frequently and are ungrateful to your husbands. I have not seen anyone more deficient in intelligence and religion than you. A cautious sensible man could be led astray by some of you."

The women asked, "O Allah's Apostle! What is deficient in our intelligence and religion?"

He said, "Is not the evidence of two women equal to the witness of one man?" [Surah 2:282]

They replied in the affirmative.

He said, "This is the deficiency in her intelligence. Isn't it true that a woman can neither pray nor fast during her menses?"

The women replied in the affirmative.

He said, "This is the deficiency in her religion."[3]

This story says two things about women:

1. Women aren't as intelligent as men. That's why it takes the testimony of two women in court to equal one man:

And get two witnesses out of your own men. And if there are not two men (available), then a man and two women, such as you agree for witnesses, so that if one of them (two women) errs, the other can remind her.

—Surah 2:282, Muhsin Khan

Here's what a modern Muslim scholar concludes:

The mental ability of woman cannot reach the mental ability of a man. This is what the scholars agree, and it is very familiar to them.[4]

2. Women aren't as holy as men.

When a woman can't pray or fast because of her period, she must make up the missed duties on other days. Even if she does this, Muhammad tells her that in the eyes of Allah she is still "deficient in her religion."

Muhammad also said a woman's presence would cancel the prayer of a man, meaning he would have to start over the *raka'ah* he had been praying. His wife Aisha said:

> The things which annul prayer were mentioned before me (and those were): a dog, a donkey and a woman.[5]

Two women equal one man.

The value of men compared to women is also demonstrated in the Quranic revelation about inheritance. The Quran says:

> If there are brethren, men and women, then the male shall have the like of the portion of two females.
>
> —Surah 4:176, SHAKIR

In terms of women, this version says that a brother should get twice as much of an inheritance as his sister. You can argue that men were supporting the women of society, so they needed more money. That may be a valid argument, but the Quran also says two female witnesses equal one male witness:

> And call to witness, from among your men, two witnesses. And if two men be not (at hand) then a man and two women.
>
> —Surah 2:282, PICKTHAL

Taking both verses into consideration, Muslims draw an inevitable conclusion: two women are worth one man.

Women are ungrateful.

As you'll learn in the next chapter, Muhammad had a tumultuous relationship with his wives in Medina. In this account from his famous Night Journey, you can imagine him complaining that his wives were unfaithful.

The Prophet said: "I was shown the Hell-fire and that the majority of its dwellers were women who were ungrateful." It was asked, "Do they disbelieve in Allah?" (or are they ungrateful to Allah?) He replied, "They are ungrateful to their husbands and are ungrateful for the favors and the good (charitable deeds) done to them. If you have always been good (benevolent) to one of them and then she sees something in you (not of her liking), she will say, 'I have never received any good from you.'"[6]

So Muhammad complained that wives are ungrateful for the good that their husbands do and focus on the faults.

Even the most peaceful scholars of Islam will accept these negative stereotypes about women. Imam Ghazali is the famous Islamic scholar who championed the Sufi movement, the most peaceful movement ever established in Islamic history. Sufis don't believe in jihad as physical fighting; they believe the real meaning of jihad is a spiritual struggle. He wrote about women:

There are three things that if you are going to treat them well, they will treat you badly, and one of them is woman.[7]

Women are toys.

Truly, few things would be more insulting to a modern woman than to be called a toy. Yet this was a common attitude in Muslim Arabia. An Islamic scholar reports:

The prophet Muhammad said that a woman is nothing but a toy, and if someone has a woman, he has to take care of her.[8]

Muhammad's followers carried the same attitude:

> One day Umar [Umar ibn al-Khattib, the second successor of Muhammad] was speaking, and a woman interrupted him, and he said to her, "Woman, you have nothing to do. You are just like a toy, and if we need you, we will call you.[9]

Ordinary Muslims today hardly ever hear hadith like this, and if they do they will have a hard time believing they are for real. On the other hand, when a committed Muslim hears something like this, he checks the sources. He will recognize that the source is one of the well-known writers in the Middle East about Muslim affairs—not a non-Muslim writing against Islam. So the committed Muslim will accept this hadith.

Women are an affliction.

Muhammad also described women as an "affliction":

> The Prophet said, "After me I have not left any affliction more harmful to men than women."[10]

Muhammad compared women to a crooked rib:

> Allah's Apostle said, "The woman is like a rib; if you try to straighten her, she will break. So if you want to get benefit from her, do so while she still has some crookedness."[11]

Muhammad meant that women are flawed (crooked) but weak (they will break if you bend them). He seemed to be saying that it was best to leave a woman alone and not try to make her better.

Women are a source of evil.

> I heard the Prophet saying. "Evil omen is in three things:
> The horse, the woman and the house."[12]

An omen is a sign of a future event. For example, if someone in the Middle East opens his front door to go outside and he sees a black bird flying in the air and calling, he expects something bad is going to open. The bird is a bad omen.

Muhammad said that the horse, the woman, and the house were bad omens. Why these three things? Muhammad came from Bedouin people who lived in tents. They weren't comfortable with houses, so houses were a bad omen to them. The horse was a bad omen because horses brought war, killing, and death. The woman was a bad omen because she was a woman.

A Few Good Words

Muhammad presented a degrading and negative stereotype of women. But on the other hand, he also made comments that encouraged men to treat women well, especially their mothers.

Another popular teaching about women also comes from the hadith:

> A man asked Muhammad, "Who deserves my obedience?"
>
> And Muhammad said, "Your mother."
> The man said, "Who?"
> Muhammad answered, "Your mother."
> For the third time, the man asked who?
> Muhammad said, "Your mother.
> The fourth time the man asked, "Who?," Muhammad answered, "Your father."

Imams use this little story to teach that the mother should be obeyed and honored.

The Quran says:

> And We have enjoined on man to be dutiful and kind
> to his parents. His mother bears him with hardship and
> she brings him forth with hardship...
> —Surah 46:15, MUHSIN KHAN

Even today, Muslim people always repeat Muhammad's famous saying: "Paradise is under the feet of the mother." Muslim society uses this comment to say that all women are valuable, not just mothers.

As I mentioned earlier, men are also told to take responsibility for women: "Men are the protectors and maintainers of women" (Surah 4:34, MUHSIN KHAN).

So despite all the negative attitudes about women, imams can use other teachings about women to tell society to treat women with respect and kindness.

Ten
ISLAMIC LAW ABOUT MARRIAGE

IN A PASSIONATE AND VOLATILE SOCIETY LIKE ARABIA IN THE seventh century, marriages were also passionate and volatile. Husbands and wives would argue bitterly, get divorced, and then come back together again. Muhammad's own marriages to his thirteen wives were equally tumultuous.

In order to understand how women are viewed, it's important to understand the role of the woman as a wife. We will begin by looking at Muhammad's relationships with his wives and how this affected the laws that developed to regulate marriage in Muslim society.

Muhammad's Wives

In the first eleven years of Muhammad's revelation, he was married to only one woman, Khadija, until her death. She was a woman of good standing in society who staunchly supported Muhammad's revelations.

But after Khadija's death, the girl he married was a totally different picture. I call her a girl because she was only a girl when she became engaged to Muhammad. Many Muslims do not realize how young she really was. According to the Correct Book of Bukhari, the most respected book of hadith, Muhammad was engaged to her when she was six and consummated the marriage when she was nine.[1]

This girl was named Aisha, and she stayed with Muhammad as his favorite wife until his death when she was eighteen years old. During their marriage, Aisha was accused of adultery, and there is a long passage about this incident in the Quran. (See Surah 42:11–18.) I believe this caused Muhammad to be insecure about women.

However, Muhammad did not stop his relationship with women when he married Aisha. After the death of Khadija, it seems that the floodgates of marriage were opened for him.

Sometimes Muhammad looked to see who was the most beautiful lady or girl being taken as a prisoner of war, and he would take her to be one of his wives. One of the famous ladies he got that way was a Jewish girl named Safiya bint Ho-yay. Another one was a Jewish woman named Juwayriya bint al-Harith. Ultimately, after Khadija, he married another twelve women.

These women constantly postured among themselves about who would spend time with the prophet. They complained about Aisha getting more nights than the other wives. They complained about not having enough money. One time Muhammad threatened to divorce all of them.[2]

Muhammad's Female Slaves

Islamic law provides for the position of a wife, but there is also something called *amah*, meaning "slave." Almost every Muslim of Muhammad's time had women as slaves. Why? Because during Muhammad's time, women were like products in the market to be bought and sold. Also, every time you went to war against another group, the prisoners of war—women or girls—became slaves. They were divided among the Muslim soldiers.

So if you visited the men of Medina in their homes, you would not see just one woman. You would see plenty of women, but you would recognize differences between them. You would see one lady had more power and influence in the house because she was a wife. And you would see another one who was like a maid in the house. She was treated like a maid and dressed like a maid, not a wife.

Even today, if you visit some houses in Saudi Arabia, you will see the same picture. They don't have slaves as they did during Muhammad's time, but they have ladies from Sri Lanka and the Philippines who live in the houses like maids, and the husband uses them as he wishes.

Under Islamic law, a Muslim man has the right to a sexual relationship with his female slave, but she is not considered his wife and she cannot carry his name. She has no right to inherit anything of his wealth. She cannot be in the same position as one of his wives. If he has kids from her, these kids belong to her, not to him. They will never carry his name; they will carry their mother's name. So the child would not be called Mustafa, the son of Muhammad, for example. The child would be called Mustafa, son of Fatima or Maria. Muhammad had twenty-three female slaves.[3]

Keeping Muhammad's relationships with his wives and female slaves in mind, let's look at what Islamic law says about marriage, sex, and divorce.

The Ideal Marriage

The nicest verse in the Quran about husbands and wives is Surah 30:21 (ALI), which says:

> And among His Signs is this, that He created for you mates from among yourselves, that ye may dwell in tranquility with them, and He has put love and mercy between your (hearts): verily in that are Signs for those who reflect.

Muslims always put this verse on wedding invitations and use it during the weddings. This is the only verse like it in the entire Quran. The other verses in the Quran about marriage focus on how to deal with problems, like disobedient wives, and the regulations for getting a divorce.

Husbands Disciplining Wives

In the previous chapter, we looked at the first part of Surah 4:34, which said that men are the protectors and guardians of women. The second part of the verse tells what the Muslim man may do if his wife disobeys him (ALI):

> As to those women on whose part ye fear disloyalty and ill-conduct, admonish them (first), (Next), refuse to share their beds, (And last) beat them (lightly); but if they return to obedience, seek not against them Means (of annoyance).

It's a three-step process. First, admonish. Second, refuse to share their beds. Third, beat them lightly.

Liberal women in the Muslim world have vigorously examined this verse and offered mediating explanations about the beating. I agree with these women that no man should beat his wife, and I hope that these women bring about a change in Muslim society. However, I think the women will have a great challenge, because even if they can change the application of this verse, the general picture of women in the Quran and hadith will not be affected.

Passion for Sexuality

Arabian society had a passion for sexuality, and men would boast about their sexual stamina. Most Muslims do not realize that the hadith has several anecdotes about Muhammad's sexual stamina. For example:

> The Prophet used to pass by (have sexual relation with) all his wives in one night, and at that time he had nine wives.[4]

> He said the apostle of Allah said, "Allah has given me the power of forty men in having sex."[5]

Muhammad's followers also kept company with multiple women. Ali was the most religious person around Muhammad in his time, and he was living with four official wives and seventeen concubines.[6]

This love of sex is reflected in the teachings about paradise, where men will enjoy sex with virgins for eternity. (See Surah 52:20.)

In Islamic tradition, there is even a prayer for the husband to say before he and his wife have sex. If he doesn't say this prayer, he believes that Satan can have sex with his wife. The words are: "Oh, Allah, protect me from Satan. And take Satan away from what you have given to me [meaning his wife]." The committed Muslims will follow this practice. Even the position of the husband and the wife during intercourse is discussed in the Quran. (See Surah 2:223.)

Divorce Laws in the Quran

In Muslim and Arabian society, divorce was commonly practiced. As far as I know, Muhammad didn't change the practices of Arabian society significantly.

It's only speculation on my part, but even though Muhammad thought of women as inferior, I think he enjoyed their company and did not want to see Muslim women treated unfairly. The Islamic laws for divorce still keep the man in a superior position over the woman, but they also call for the man not to mistreat the woman or leave her destitute.

As always, Islamic law looks first to the Quran for examples. Then additional clarification is obtained from the life of Muhammad. In this chapter, we will follow the same pattern.

The Quran teaches about divorce mainly in two chapters. Surah 65, which is appropriately titled "The Divorce," defines waiting periods. Surah 2, called "The Cow," defines fair treatment for divorced women, including support or a one-time gift. Here are some details from those passages.

There must be a waiting period before a divorce is finalized.

The verses in Surah 65 describe a waiting period between the time the husband declares he is divorcing a wife and the time that she actually leaves his house and they are divorced. If the wife has regular menses, then the husband should try to divorce her when she is not having her menses; the waiting period will end when she has finished her next menses and is clean again. At the end of the waiting period, the husband may decide to keep his wife or they may "part with them in a good manner" (Surah 65:2, Muhsin Khan).

Naturally, the Muslim community needed information for other possible scenarios. So the passage goes on to explain that if the wife does not have her menses because she is too old or too young, then the waiting period is three months. (See Surah 65:4.)

If the wife is pregnant, the divorce is not finalized until after the pregnancy.

If the wife is pregnant when the husband declares his intention to divorce, the waiting period lasts until she is no longer pregnant, and the husband must support her while she is pregnant. When the child is born, the baby will belong to the husband. After the birth, he may choose to finalize the divorce with his wife, but he may still pay her to nurse his child for him. The husband's other option is to keep the child and find another woman to nurse the baby. (See Surah 65:6.)

Husbands have more rights in the divorce process than wives.

> And the divorced women should keep themselves in waiting for three courses; and it is not lawful for them that they should conceal what Allah has created in their wombs, if they believe in Allah and the last day; and their husbands have a better right to take them back in the meanwhile if they wish for reconciliation; and they have rights similar to those against them in a just manner, and the men are *a degree above them*, and Allah is Mighty, Wise.
> —Surah 2:228, SHAKIR, emphasis added

This verse says matter-of-factly that men are "a degree above" women during the divorce process.

Husbands should not keep a wife in order to mistreat her.

> When ye divorce women, and they fulfill the term of their ('Iddat) [waiting period], either take them back on equitable terms or set them free on equitable terms; but do not take them back to injure them, (or) to take

undue advantage; if any one does that; He wrongs his own soul.

—Surah 2:231, ALI

If the husband has not consummated the marriage with the wife, he may divorce her but must pay her a one-time gift.

If you divorce women while yet you have not touched them...bestow on them a gift of reasonable amount.

—Surah 2:236, MUHSIN KHAN

Husbands must pay maintenance for the wives they divorce.

And for the divorced women, maintenance (should be provided) on reasonable (scale).

—Surah 2:241, MUHSIN KHAN

Divorce Law in the Hadith

When you read about divorce in the hadith, you get a picture of the volatile and intense nature of relationships in that society.[7]

For example, imagine a husband and wife have an argument. The husband finally gets angry and says to his wife, "I divorce you," one time. Later he realizes that he doesn't want a divorce. Islamic law says that he may go back to her and be reconciled.

If they have another fight and he says to his wife, "I divorce you," one or two times during that argument, he can still change his mind and be reconciled with her.

However, if they have a disastrous conflict and he says, "I divorce you," three times, then Islamic law says they cannot reconcile except under one condition—the woman must marry another man and be divorced before she can be reconciled to the first husband.[8]

This teaching is commonly understood among ordinary

Muslims, and people are actually careful about what words they use when they fight.

A husband is permitted to divorce his wife for a wide variety of reasons—both trivial and serious. He can divorce her because she has been unfaithful and slept with another man, but he can also divorce her simply because they argue a lot or they have had a serious disagreement. Sometimes the divorce happens because she cannot have children. The husband may say to his wife, "I am going to take another wife so that she can give me children." If the first wife objects and says, "I can't live with another woman in the house," then he may just decide to divorce her.

Under Islamic law, a woman does not have the same right to initiate a divorce as a man. But she does have the right of *al-khula*, meaning that she can divorce her husband if he is not worthy to be a husband any longer according to Islamic law. The principle would apply if the husband chose to leave Islam and follow another religion or if he became disabled in a way that would keep him from being a husband and father, like being in a coma. *Al-khula* cannot be invoked for incompatibility or minor issues. It has to be something really serious. In short, Islamic law says divorce is the right of the man, and *al-khula* is the right of the woman.

In the past, a Muslim woman did not have the right to initiate a divorce. But the secular governments in the Islamic world are passing some laws to give women the right to ask for a divorce if she is in danger. Little changes are happening here and there.

Conclusion

Islamic law makes man superior. This does not mean every man abuses his wife or gives his wife a hard time. Ordinary Muslims treat their wives much better than the men in Muhammad's day. They have never heard some of the verses you have read in this chapter. The committed Muslim is different. He knows most of this material, and his attitude toward women is affected.

Eleven
WOMEN'S RIGHTS UNDER ISLAM

THERE IS ONE AREA WHERE WOMEN ARE EQUAL WITH MEN under Islam—in their responsibility to fulfill the duties of Islam. The woman may have to cover her body in the street and get permission to travel, but she must still pray five times a day, fast for Ramadan, take the pilgrimage to Mecca if she can, and give alms for the poor if she wants to enter into paradise:

> And whoso doeth good works, whether of male or female, and he (or she) is a believer, such will enter paradise and they will not be wronged the dint in a date-stone.
>
> —Surah 4:124, PICKTHAL

A woman also has the duty of jihad. Some of the women during Muhammad's day participated in jihad, traveling with the army and treating the wounded:

> A woman came and stayed at the palace of Bani Khalaf and she narrated about her sister whose husband took part in twelve holy battles along with the Prophet and her sister was with her husband in six (out of these twelve). She (the woman's sister) said, "We used to treat the wounded, look after patients.[1]

Committed Muslim women today also feel the call of jihad. I witnessed this myself when I lived in Egypt.

Radical Muslim Women

When I lived in Cairo, I always bought my groceries at the same little store, which was owned by a committed Muslim. He wore a beard, and his wife covered herself. When I saw him one day, he seemed a little bit sad, so I asked, "What's happening with you?"

He said, "My wife left me and went back to her family, and she doesn't want to come back to my house again."

I asked, "Why?"

He said, "She is not satisfied with the way I am serving Allah."

I asked again, "Why?"

He answered, "She said to me, 'Why don't you join one of the Islamist groups and fight for the way of Allah and defend the religion? You love money more than Allah, and I don't want this.'"

I said to him, "So she left you to live with her family because you are not willing to go and kill yourself. So she wants to kill you? Do you want to live with someone like this? Is she the right wife?"

He answered sadly, "She exceeds me in her commitment to Allah."

When a Muslim woman becomes committed to Islam, it will impact her life. She will learn how women functioned during the life of Muhammad and his first successor. The women joined the military and fought side by side with the men, took care of the injured soldiers, or supplied them with food and ammunition.

There is a famous story in Islamic history about a woman named Al-Khansa who had four sons. The call of jihad came, and the first son went out and was killed on the battlefield. The call of jihad came again, and the second son went out and was killed. The third son was also killed, and finally the fourth. When she received the news of the death of her fourth son, she said, "I thank Allah for honoring me by the death of my sons, and if I have another son I will offer him to Allah." In 1994, Al-Qaeda actually launched a magazine named after Al-Khansa with the purpose of encouraging Muslim women to participate in jihad.[2]

Stories like these push the committed Muslim woman toward becoming a radical. Deep inside she wants to live the right way for Allah.

Dr. Qaradawi, the most influential Sunni scholar in the world today, said there is no difference between man and woman when it comes to the duty of jihad.

Here's how he answered this question posed by a man named Abul Fedat from Morocco on November 11, 2006. Abul asked the question, "Is a woman allowed to fight in the name of Allah and kill herself and kill others with a suicide bomb?"

Dr. Qaradawi answered:

> Muslim scholars agree that when the enemies of Muslims come to the land of Islam, jihad is a must. There is no difference between the Muslim man and woman. They have to strive and fight, and they don't need permission from a spouse to do so. Children do not need permission from parents. But if the enemies have not entered the land of Muslims and the fight is outside of the land, then a woman should ask her husband's permission [before going to jihad].
>
> A woman is allowed to commit suicide, and this is one of the most good, beautiful, acceptable deeds that

can be done for Allah himself. He will appreciate it and he will reward her for that."

Qaradawi ended by quoting Surah 9:71 (ALI):

The Believers, men and women, are protectors one of another: they enjoin what is just, and forbid what is evil: they observe regular prayers, practise regular charity, and obey Allah and His Messenger. On them will Allah pour His mercy: for Allah is Exalted in power, Wise.

Through this legal opinion, Dr. Qaradawi made it clear to the Muslim world that women have the right to be suicide bombers.[3]

Conclusion

While women do not have equal status under Islam, they do have equal obligation to fulfill the duties of the religion, whether it is giving alms to the poor or, for radical Muslims, fighting jihad. In short, women have the same duties, but they do not have the same freedoms.

Twelve
LOSS OF FREEDOM FOR WOMEN

IN ARABIAN SOCIETY BEFORE MUHAMMAD CAME, PEOPLE believed a man could find trouble from a woman just by looking at her. This attitude easily found its way into Muslim culture. Islam tries to keep men and women separated and to limit communication between them very strictly. For example, women can attend Friday prayer at the mosque, but during the week women are encouraged to pray at home, not at the mosque. There is severe separation between males and females in schools, at celebrations, and even in homes with family members.

Women are robbed of their freedoms by the Islamic system of separation and suspicion between women and men. The system places a wall between men and women by making sure that women are:

- Covered
- Restricted from traveling

In the good families in the Middle East, a woman has dignity and respect from her husband, children, extended family, and neighborhood, but she doesn't have her freedom.

Why Women Should Be Covered

When I was growing up in Egypt during the 1960s and 1970s, my home and community tried to follow the example of Muhammad literally in all areas of life, including the relationship between men and women. Even in my home, my mother was always covered. I was in my late twenties before I saw my mother's hair for the first time. Any time she came out of her bedroom, her hair was covered. What kind of a system prohibits a little boy from seeing his own mother's hair?

Dr. Sayyid Ramadan al-Bhuti, one of the most famous Islamic scholars of modern history, gives a twofold reason behind the covering: (1) to protect women from men, and (2) to protect men from women.[1] How does the covering do this? The covering protects women by making them unattractive so that they will not be attacked by men. It protects men by making women unattractive so men won't commit sin with them.

The bottom line is that women need to be covered because they are a temptation for men to sin. The covering solves a problem that is in the man, not in the woman.

This logic is evident in the verse from the Quran that calls for women to be covered, which says:

> O Prophet! Tell thy wives and daughters, and the believing women, that they should cast their outer garments over their persons (when abroad): that is most convenient, that they should be known (as such) and not molested. And Allah is Oft-Forgiving, Most Merciful.
>
> —Surah 33:59, ALI

In other words, women should cover up so they will not be molested.

During one of his sermons, the imam of the largest mosque in Sydney, Australia, asked why society always blames the man when a woman gets raped or attacked. He said:

> It is she who takes off her clothes, shortens them, flirts, puts on makeup and powder and takes to the streets, God protect us, dallying.... But when it comes to this

disaster, who started it?…If she had not left the meat uncovered, the cat wouldn't have snatched it.[2]

This statement created a huge reaction in Australia. The prime minister condemned him, and the Islamic community removed him as leader of the mosque. I'm proud that the government and the Muslims in Australia did not tolerate this evil attitude toward women.

How Women Should Be Covered

Since the Quran says women must be covered, the next step is to decide exactly how much needs to be covered. The Quran gives a general description but not complete details. For example:

> And say to the believing women that they should lower their gaze and guard their modesty; that they should not display their beauty and ornaments except what (must ordinarily) appear thereof; that they should draw their veils over their bosoms and not display their beauty.
>
> —Surah 24:31, ALI

However, the hadith gives more information, which has been interpreted by the four schools of Islamic law. Two of these schools of law, Malik and Abi Hanifa, permit a woman to uncover her face and hands, but she must not wear makeup or embellishments. Dr. Bhuti's book explains:

> Muslim scholars agree that nothing should be uncovered from a woman except her face and her hands under a specific condition. It has to be her hand and face in normal condition, no makeup or embellishment.[3]

But Muslims who believe in the legal school of thought called Hanbal and some of the people who are following the school of Shafa'a say women are not allowed to uncover their face, hair, or hands, meaning they have to cover all the body.[4]

As a result, you can go down the street in a Muslim country and see one woman wearing a *hijab* with her face and hands uncovered and in the next block see a woman wearing a *hijab* that covers everything, including her face and hands, and all you can see are her eyes through the slit in her head covering.

In modern times, however, a Muslim woman might refuse to wear the *hijab*. If her husband is traditional, he will be quite concerned about this. He will think, "I know the prophet said that if a woman leaves her house without *hijab*, the angels will curse her until she comes back. And I know that the prophet saw many women punished in hell in his Night Journey because they weren't obedient to Allah. I am worried about the disobedience of my wife to Allah and to Islamic law in not fulfilling the duty of wearing *hijab*."

One of his moderate friends might say, "Does she pray five times a day? Does she fast Ramadan month? If she is loving and kind and obedient to you and to Allah, why not just be patient? Maybe Allah will open her eyes and help her to see that this is very important for her to wear *hijab*."

But the friend who is a really committed Muslim will say to him, "You know what? You have to show her that this is really disobeying Allah and that this is a sign that she is in rebellion against putting Islam into practice completely in her life. She is believing in some and rejecting the other. [See Surah 4:150–151.] The Quran is clear on this issue. You have to threaten her by giving her only two options: wear the *hijab* or get a divorce."

Travel Outside the Home Restricted

Islamic law says a woman cannot leave her house without permission from her husband. People in the Muslim world always quote Muhammad as saying, "If a woman goes out of her house without permission from her husband, the angel of Allah will curse her until she comes back home."

A woman can't leave the country without a *dhu-mahram* as a protector, who is usually a husband, brother, or father:

> The Prophet said, "A woman should not travel except with a Dhu-Mahram (her husband or a man with whom that woman cannot marry at all according to the Islamic Jurisprudence), and no man may visit her except in the presence of a Dhu-Mahram."[5]

After Muhammad said this, a Muslim man stood up and asked Muhammad about a specific circumstance. The man said he was planning to go fight with a certain army, but his wife wanted to perform *hajj*, meaning that she would need to travel to Mecca and Medina. Muhammad told the man, "Go with your wife to *hajj*."

Islamic legal scholars say that if Muhammad didn't want women to travel without a *dhu-mahram* to *hajj*, then women certainly cannot travel outside the country without one.

Another hadith says, "No lady should travel without her husband or without a *Dhu-Mahram* for a two-days' journey."[6] So the restrictions on travel are stated clearly.

Visitors to the Home Restricted

Islamic law also says a woman cannot be alone with a male that she could marry:

> He heard the Prophet saying, "It is not permissible for a
> man to be alone with a woman."[7]

If I were married and my wife were at home alone, my brother would not be allowed to visit her. That's because my wife could marry my brother if she were not married to me. But my dad could visit her, because even if she were divorced from me, she could not marry him because she was the wife of his son. Regulations for other relatives are explained in great detail in Surah 4, "The Women."

If my wife had someone with her at the house, like a sister or girlfriend, then it would be OK for her to allow a man, such as my brother, to come inside the house. The point is to avoid having a man and woman alone together.

The rules for being together in a house also apply to being together in other places, such as a car. I read a sad story related to this issue on the BBC Arabic news Web site. A newspaper interviewed a nineteen-year-old woman who had been raped in Saudi Arabia:

> The 19-year-old said she was blackmailed a year ago into meeting a man who threatened to tell her family they were having a relationship outside wedlock, which is illegal in the ultra-conservative desert kingdom.
>
> After driving off together from a shopping mall near her home, the woman and the man were stopped and abducted by a gang of men wielding kitchen knives who took them to a farm where she was raped 14 times by her captors.
>
> Five men were arrested for the rape and given jail terms ranging from 10 months to five years.[8]

The rape victim also had a trial, and the court sentenced her to ninety lashes. Why did they do that? Because she was sitting in a car with a man and there was no person from her family with them. She had violated Islamic law.

Because of her ordeal, this woman tried to commit suicide. Her younger brother beat her because the rape had brought shame on their family. This girl is a victim of Islamic law.

Women Cannot Lead Men

Under the Islamic system, a woman should not take a leadership position in society. Muhammad said in hadith:

> Never will succeed such a nation as makes a woman their ruler.[9]

Women who lead human rights groups in Egypt have had big discussions in the newspaper about this hadith, saying that it is not correct or accurate. Their cause received a setback when Dr. Yusef Qaradawi gave a legal opinion about it.

As I said earlier, Dr. Qaradawi is the top Sunni scholar in our modern times and president of the Worldwide Muslim Society of Scholars. On his Web site, www.qaradawi.net, he gives legal opinions as a qualified Muslim scholar. I took some classes with Dr. Qaradawi when he was a professor at Al-Azhar. When Dr. Qaradawi gave an opinion about this hadith, it was a significant event. He wrote:

> This hadith is correct and it is narrated by Abu Bakr, the first successor after Muhammad. Muhammad said this hadith when he heard the people of Persia [Iran] gave leadership in their nation to the daughter of the former king and she became like a queen of Persia.[10]

So Dr. Qaradawi sided with tradition and declared that Allah is truly against women becoming leaders.

Conclusion

The teachings of Islam declare that all men are *not* created equal. For example, the Muslim is always higher than the non-Muslim, and the man is superior to the woman. Changing these ideas would mean changing the interpretation of the Quran.

One of the fundamental principles of freedom in the United States says the opposite. Thomas Jefferson wrote in the Declaration of Independence:

> We hold these truths to be self-evident, that all men are
> created equal, that they are endowed by their Creator
> with certain unalienable Rights, that among these are
> Life, Liberty and the pursuit of Happiness.

"All men are created equal"—what a powerful phrase, even though it wasn't fully practiced for almost 150 years. It wasn't until 1870 and the passing of the fifteenth amendment that freed slaves were guaranteed the right to vote, and it wasn't until 1920 that the nineteenth amendment gave women the right to vote.

But the point I'd like to make is that the United States could make these changes and increase "liberty and justice for all" without violating any religious law. The government had the freedom to debate the issue and change culture. The Muslim world does not have this freedom as long as religion and politics are tangled together. For real progress to be made, religion and politics need to be untangled.

In the next section of this book I will give you a dramatic

look at how the laws of the Islamic world are affected by the tangle of religion and politics. You will be amazed by the difference between Islamic law and the laws that are practiced in America and the West.

SECTION IV

THE CLASH BETWEEN ISLAMIC CULTURE AND AMERICAN LAW

Thirteen
SEVEN WAYS ISLAMIC LAW CLASHES WITH WESTERN LAW

ISLAMIC CULTURE IS ESTABLISHED IN SUCH A POWERFUL WAY because it is defined by Islamic law. These are not traditions that are passed down from generation to generation, being adapted and modified to changing times and conditions. These are laws that were established in the seventh century and are maintained in their original form.

If you ask the Muslims of Egypt, "Do you support an Islamic state in Egypt or do you want a secular, liberal government?" more than 80 percent will say that they want Islamic government to rule with Islamic law. They look at Islam as the answer for their daily problems. They may lose some of their freedom, but they prefer Islam to rule.

The question to ask, therefore, is, What does Islamic law look like? Is it similar to the laws that are in place in the West?

In this chapter I will take you to Medina, the historical capital of Islam and the birthplace of sharia law, and also where Muhammad lived for a little more than ten years before he died there. We will find Malik or Omar or Abu Bakr and ask them to tell us how sharia law deals with different crimes.

When we hear their answers, we are going to compare them to American rights and freedoms. If Islam ever ruled America, you and the rest of the American people would be living under sharia. You can decide if this would be a pretty picture or a nightmare that you would wish to disappear forever.

First, here are some basics about sharia law. Islamic law has four main schools of thought, but all are in agreement that the highest authority for law under Islam is the Quran. So any judgment expressed in the Quran must be accepted and cannot be abrogated by any other source. For areas not addressed in the Quran, the legal scholars turn to the example of Muhammad for guidance. For areas not addressed by Muhammad's life, the legal scholars look to Islamic history. For areas not addressed in history, the scholars must use logic, reasoning, and discussion among themselves to come to a decision as a group. This process is known as *ijma'ah*, literally meaning "a group in agreement."

In the study that follows, I will concentrate on law that is based in the Quran. This will avoid gray areas about how to interpret the hadith. For an overview of this chapter, please see the chart on the following two pages that lists key laws and the important facts about them.

Crime	Description	References in the Quran	Islamic Punishment	American Punishment	Principle in Conflict
Rebellion against the Muslim leader	This can be physical rebellion or verbal rebellion	Surah 5:33	Death or exile	Jail, execution (rarely)	Freedom of speech (first amendment)
Apostasy	A Muslim who decides to leave Islam	Surah 4:88–89	Three days to repent; if no repentance, then death	None	Freedom of religion
Adultery	Sex between single persons	Surah 24:2	Beaten with 100 lashes	None	Cruel and unusual punishment
	Sex between persons not married to each other	The Correct Book of Muslim, bk. 17, no. 4206	Death by stoning		

Crime	Description	References in the Quran	Islamic Punishment	American Punishment	Principle in Conflict
Alcohol	Drinking alcohol, using intoxicants	Surah 5:90–91; 2:219; Book of Muslim, bk. 17, no. 4226	Beaten with eighty lashes	None (The U.S. prohibition of alcohol lasted from 1920–1933)	Cruel and unusual punishment
Stealing	Stealing of any amount, even just a quarter of a dinar	Surah 5:38	Right hand cut off at the wrist	Jail, paying for damages	Cruel and unusual punishment
Slander	Telling a lie that hurts someone's reputation	Surah 24:13	Beaten with eighty lashes	Monetary damages assesed	Cruel and unusual punishment
Murder	Killing someone outside of war	Surah 2:178	Equal life for equal life; a Muslim cannot be killed for murdering a non-Muslim, woman, or slave	Jail, execution	All men are created equal

1. Rebellion Against the Muslim Leader (Treason)

Principle in conflict: freedom of speech, definition of treason

Rebellion has a broad definition in Islamic law: it is disobedience against the *amir* (Islamic leader) in action or by word. In other words, rebellion can be as dramatic as assembling an army and declaring war or as subtle as speaking critical words against the *amir*. It is considered to be one of the biggest crimes in Islamic law.

The punishment for this crime is graphically described by the Quran:

> The punishment of those who wage war against Allah and His Messenger, and strive with might and main for mischief through the land is: execution, or crucifixion, or the cutting off of hands and feet from opposite sides, or exile from the land: that is their disgrace in this world, and a heavy punishment is theirs in the Hereafter.
>
> —Surah 5:33, ALI

Muhammad demonstrated that the punishment was the same for physical uprising or verbal attacks, such as writing poetry or preaching to others to convince them not to follow Muhammad.

Muhammad feared rebellion by word more than physical rebellion. One rebel movement was led by a woman named al-Assmah, who was writing poetry against Muhammad and his revelation. When Muhammad saw the threat of her message, he became so fearful of her that he asked his friends one day, "Who can be for Assmah?" In other words, he asked, "Who will go and kill Assmah?"

Some of his friends answered his call, and they carried out Muhammad's judgment and killed this woman who had no weapons or underground terrorist group. All she did was speak out with words and poetry.

There was another poet who was less dangerous to Muhammad than this woman. He was a Jewish man named Ka'ab ibn al-Ashraf. Muhammad also asked a group of his friends, "Who will kill Ka'ab ibn al-Ashraf? He has maligned Allah, the Exalted, and His Messenger."

A man named Muhammad ibn Maslama volunteered. The way he handled the assassination makes for an interesting story. Pretending that he needed some money, Maslama asked al-Ashraf for a loan. The poet agreed as long as Maslama brought him some weapons as collateral.

The next night Maslama returned with accomplices. When al-Ashraf came down, the men said to him, "We sense from you a very fine smell."

He said, "Yes, I have with me a mistress who is the most scented of the women of Arabia."

Maslama said, "Allow me to smell the scent on your head."

Al-Ashraf said, "Yes, you may smell."

So Maslama held him by the head and smelled. He let go and said, "Allow me to do so (once again)."

This time he held the poet's head fast and said to his companions: "Do your job." And they killed him.[1]

Muhammad justified the assassination by saying, "If he [the poet] had stayed silent just as everyone who shared his same opinion stayed, he wouldn't have been murdered. But he harmed us with his poetry, and any one of you who did that would have deserved the sword."[2]

This woman and this man didn't keep what they believed about Muhammad to themselves; they tried to influence other people as well. This is why Muhammad considered them to be fighting against Allah and carried out judgment against them.

These are not obscure stories that ordinary Muslims have never heard; they are commonly used during Friday sermons. Ordinary people may not remember all the details of how the killing was carried out, but they definitely know the stories in general.

Cartoon controversy

The Muslim world is hypersensitive toward anything that appears to be a criticism of Islam. On September 30, 2005, a Danish newspaper published some cartoon drawings that criticized Muhammad. For example, one cartoon showed Muhammad with a lit bomb on his head instead of a turban. The Muslim world was outraged, launched a boycott of Danish products, and erupted in riots where dozens of people died. A reward was offered to anyone who would kill the publisher of the newspaper or the cartoonist.

Was the outcry about drawing an image of Muhammad? No. Even though Sunni tradition forbids making an image of Muhammad, there have been many printed images of Muhammad in the West that caused no protest. The problem is that the cartoons criticized Muhammad.

Muslim leaders demanded an apology from the government of Denmark, which was refused. I completely support Denmark's position. I believe the media in Denmark should only answer to the laws of Denmark, not the laws of Islam. Muslims living in Western countries cannot impose Islamic law on Western life and culture. If Muslims in the West want to follow Islamic law, they should go back to their Islamic countries and enjoy Islamic law there.

The people of the free world must refuse to lay down their freedoms due to Islamic intimidation.

Rebellion in America

Islamic law about rebellion conflicts with the U.S. Constitution in two ways. First, the Constitution has a very limited definition of treason. It says in article 3, section 3:

> Treason against the United States, shall consist only in levying War against them, or in adhering to their Enemies, giving them Aid and Comfort. No Person shall be convicted of Treason unless on the Testimony of two Witnesses to the same overt Act, or on Confession in open Court.

Criticizing the government is not treason. Treason means making war or assisting an enemy. Americans can criticize their government all they want—and they certainly use this freedom energetically.

Second, Islamic law demolishes the first amendment of the U.S. Constitution, which says, "Congress shall make no law...abridging freedom of speech." Government shall make "no law." This is the highest possible protection of speech.

Think about sharia law being implemented in the United States, not far away in the hot sands of the Middle East. Imagine if the president were a Muslim and America were an Islamic state. Imagine the media starting to speak negatively about the president, trying to convince the people to vote against his party in the next election. How could the president and his party respond?

According to Islamic law, these people would fall under the crime of rebellion against the *amir*. Their punishment would be execution, crucifixion, disfigurement, or exile. (See

Surah 5:33.) Imagine how many Americans could be killed for this crime!

2. Apostasy—Leaving Islam

Principle in conflict: freedom of religion

Apostasy under Islamic law refers to a Muslim man or woman who decides to leave Islam and go back to his or her previous religion or to believe in something else. Islamic law describes this crime as betraying the religion, and the Quran establishes a severe punishment:

> They long that ye should disbelieve even as they disbelieve, that ye may be upon a level (with them). So choose not friends from them till they forsake their homes in the way of Allah; if they turn back (to enmity) then take them and kill them wherever ye find them, and choose no friend nor helper from among them.
>
> —Surah 4:89, PICKTHAL

In context, it is clear that those who "disbelieve" in this verse are people who accepted Islam and then turned away. In the first part of the verse, the Muslim community is told to reject apostates as friends unless the apostates decide to leave their homes and go back to Islam. The second half of the verse says that if the apostates refuse to return to Islam, then the Muslims should "kill them wherever ye find them, and choose no friend nor helper from among them."[3]

If there is any confusion, then Islamic scholars look to the hadith. Muhammad said, "Whoever changed his Islamic religion, then kill him."[4]

A person who has left Islam gets a chance to avoid the death penalty by returning to his faith. First, the Muslim leader must ask the person to repent and come back to Islam. If the person does that, there will be no punishment, but if he refuses, he has to be killed before sunset on the third day.

There is no dispute about what will happen to apostates in the life after death. The Quran says Allah will send apostates to hell. They will receive numerous punishments, detailed as follows.

Inevitable punishment

> Say (to the Rejecters): "My Lord is not uneasy because of you if ye call not on Him: But ye have indeed rejected (Him), and soon will come the inevitable (punishment)!"
>
> —Surah 25:77, ALI

Loss in the afterlife

> And whoever desires a religion other than Islam, it shall not be accepted from him, and in the hereafter he shall be one of the losers.
>
> —Surah 3:85, SHAKIR

Wrath from Allah

> Any one who, after accepting faith in Allah, utters Unbelief,—except under compulsion, his heart remaining firm in Faith—but such as open their breast to Unbelief, on them is Wrath from Allah, and theirs will be a dreadful Penalty.
>
> —Surah 16:106, ALI

Grievous penalty in the afterlife

> But those who reject Faith after they accepted it, and then go on adding to their defiance of Faith,—never will their repentance be accepted; for they are those who have (of set purpose) gone astray. As to those who reject

Faith, and die rejecting,—never would be accepted from any such as much gold as the earth contains, though they should offer it for ransom. For such is (in store) a penalty grievous, and they will find no helpers.

—Surah 3:90–91, ALI

Muslim scholars have had some debate over the judgment of apostasy for the people who leave Islam. Some say, "If the apostates keep their conversion to themselves and do not speak anything against Muhammad and his revelation, then they might have a light punishment, like just going to prison or going into exile [getting kicked out of the country]. But if they speak negatively about Islam or the prophet, they have to be killed."

Other Muslim scholars see no place for mercy. They say it doesn't matter if the apostate keeps the conversion to himself or not; the punishment is death.

If a Muslim has a son or brother who leaves Islam, he is motivated to kill him at two levels. First, the crime of apostasy is a violation of Islamic law. Second, the apostate brings shame to the family, so killing the apostate is their way of restoring the family's honor. This is called an "honor killing." The same thing happens in the case of adultery; the family is the first to carry out the judgment because the sin brought shame to the family, and killing the person restores their honor and fulfills the law.

The person in the Muslim world with the least freedom of religion is the Muslim himself. If he leaves Islam, he takes his life into his own hands. If he wants to speak out about his decision, his life is even more at risk. Christians and Jews at least have the option to keep their faith or accept Islam under Islamic law. The Muslim has no choice at all.

Law of apostasy in America

Before I migrated to the United States permanently, I received an invitation to visit the school of liberal arts at Harvard University in Cambridge, Massachusetts. When I arrived on campus, I encountered a white American lady in her late twenties, and I asked her, "Where is the school of liberal arts?"

She told me, "I'm going there. Come walk with me." She was a nice, respectful person. I walked with her with honor. She asked, "What are you doing there?"

I told her and asked her, "Are you working at the school or studying?"

She said, "I am studying for a master's degree in Buddhism."

I said to her, "Are you studying Buddhism because you want to become a missionary and teach the Buddhist people in Asia about Christianity?"

She looked at me as if I were very strange and asked, "What are you talking about?"

I said, "Aren't you a Christian studying Buddhism to reach out to Buddhist people?"

She said, "I'm not a Christian. I'm a Buddhist."

Her answer shocked me. I was quiet for a moment, trying to reorganize my thoughts. I finally said, "You know what? I am sorry if I may have offended you. I've lived most of my life in the Middle East, and all I know is that Buddhist people are only Asian, not American. And you are not Asian."

She smiled and said, "No. I am American, but I am a Buddhist. My father is a pastor in a church, actually, and my entire family is Christian." This wonderful American lady seemed to be happy about what she was doing. She didn't seem to face harassment from her family or society for her decision.

It was a powerful moment in my life to teach me about the freedom of religion in America. Before I ended the discussion with her, I said, "You know what? Your story gives me another understanding about how to be an American and how to live in this free land. If you were my sister in Egypt and you tried to leave Islam, not even to become a Buddhist, your brothers or father would kill you before anyone else. A couple of years ago in Egypt, I did the same thing you did and chose a religion different than what my family practices. I lost everything—my people, my job, my country. I lost more than thirty years of life. Even in America, the sword of the punishment of apostasy remains on my shoulder. Wherever I go I can be caught and killed for the honor of Allah."

She was touched by my story, and I believe she saw America in a way she had never experienced before.

Freedom of religion in America comes from the first amendment to the U.S. Constitution, which says, "Congress shall make no law respecting an establishment of religion." Imagine once again if Islamic law ruled America. The laws of apostasy would demolish freedom of religion.

The tragedy of the crime of apostasy and its punishment is not my tragedy alone; it is the tragedy of millions of Muslims around the world.

3. Adultery

Principle in conflict: cruel and unusual punishment

The crime of adultery can be divided into two categories:

- Sex between a man and woman who are not married

- Sex between a man and woman who are married but not to each other

Unmarried couples

Regarding the unmarried couple, the Quran says:

> The woman and the man guilty of adultery or fornication,—flog each of them with a hundred stripes: Let not compassion move you in their case, in a matter prescribed by Allah, if ye believe in Allah and the Last Day: and let a party of the Believers witness their punishment.
>
> —Surah 24:2, ALI

This passage means that if a man or woman are not married and are caught in the act of adultery, the punishment will be one hundred lashes. The sentence must be carried out without mercy, and the punishment must be carried out in public so people can see and hear it.

Couples not married to each other

Now we discuss the second category of adultery—married persons who have sex with a partner who is not their spouse. For example, if a married woman has sex with an unmarried man, she would have committed the second form of adultery.

During my Quranic interpretation class for my bachelor's degree, we learned the history behind the Quranic revelation about this crime against Islam. During Muhammad's time, a verse existed in the Quran that clearly spelled out the punishment. The Arabic transliteration is like this: "Al-sheikh [The man] wa [or] al-sheik'ha [the woman] izza [if] ze'ne'yeh [they commit adultery] far'ju'mu'hu'mah [stone them both] al-be'te [no negotiation]." In other words, this verse said, "If the married man and the married woman commit adultery, stone them to death—no negotiation."

However, you will no longer find this verse in the Quran. This verse was removed during the time of Uthman, the third caliph after Muhammad, who assembled one authorized version of the Quran and burned all other copies. We know about this event because it was recorded by the Islamic historians Ibn Kathir (d. 1373) and al-Suyuti (d. 1505). Even though Uthman deleted that verse from the Quran, it is still practiced in parts of the Islamic world today. Why? Because all the references to it in the hadith remained.

Many hadith discuss punishment for adultery and how Muhammad practiced it in his time. The most famous story is about the "woman of Makh-zum" who was caught in adultery:

> A woman came to the Messenger of Allah, may Allah bless him and grant him peace, and informed him that she had committed adultery and was pregnant. The Messenger of Allah, may Allah bless him and grant him peace, said to her, "Go away until you give birth." When she had given birth, she came to him. The Messenger of Allah, may Allah bless him and grant him peace, said to her, "Go away until you have suckled and weaned the baby." When she had weaned the baby, she came to him. He said, "Go and entrust the baby to someone." She entrusted the baby to someone and then came to him. He gave the order and she was stoned.[5]

Other accounts of this event describe the stoning in detail. Muhammad's companions dug a hole in the center of the city, and they put her inside the hole with only her head appearing above the ground. They stoned her in front of her baby, and some of her blood splashed onto one of the people who were stoning her, and he cursed her loudly. Muhammad heard him and said, "Don't curse her. She repented in a way that can fill heaven and earth."

Do you think I am exaggerating? Here is the published English translation of the part about the blood splashing onto one of the people:

> Khalid b Walid came forward with a stone which he flung at her head and there spurted blood on the face of Khalid and so he abused her. Allah's Apostle (may peace be upon him) heard his (Khalid's) curse that he had huried [*sic*] upon her. Thereupon he (the Holy Prophet) said: Khalid, be gentle. By Him in Whose Hand is my life, she has made such a repentance that even if a wrongful tax-collector were to repent, he would have been forgiven. Then giving command regarding her, he prayed over her and she was buried.[6]

The American mind-set can hardly comprehend such a scene. But for Christians it may bring to mind another story about a woman who committed adultery. The religious leaders brought her in front of Jesus, calling for her to be stoned to death according to the law of Moses. Jesus was silent for a time and then answered, "If any one of you is without sin, let him be the first to throw a stone at her." All her accusers disappeared and Jesus told her, "Go and sin no more." (See John 8:3–11.)

I am glad that America does not have Christianity as a state religion, but I can also see how some of the good things about Christianity—such as forgiveness—are a part of the culture of the American people. Christianity teaches against adultery, but it also acknowledges that human beings will never be perfect and so there is a plan for repentance and forgiveness. That fact that people can try to be holy and still sin is ignored by Islamic faith and by Muslim society in a very sad way.

Law of adultery in America

Imagine if Islamic law ruled America. How many men and women from coast to coast would be forced to stand in long lines in public squares where they would be punished? Law enforcement would have no other job but to spend the whole day punishing every adulterer to fulfill the law of Islam.

Also, the sentences in Islamic law are stuck in seventh-century Arabia. Lashes and stoning go against the eighth amendment of the U.S. Constitution, which says: "Cruel and unusual punishments [shall not be] inflicted." I am certain Americans would never accept sharia law for adultery.

4. Alcohol

Principle in conflict: cruel and unusual punishment

The Quran forbids the use of intoxicants:

> O ye who believe! Intoxicants and gambling, (dedication of) stones, and (divination by) arrows, are an abomination,—of Satan's handwork: eschew such (abomination), that ye may prosper. Satan's plan is (but) to excite enmity and hatred between you, with intoxicants and gambling, and hinder you from the remembrance of Allah, and from prayer: will ye not then abstain?
>
> —Surah 5:90–91, ALI

> They ask thee concerning wine and gambling. Say: "In them is great sin, and some profit, for men; but the sin is greater than the profit."
>
> —Surah 2:219, ALI

The punishment for drinking alcohol is not given in the Quran, but it is easy to find in the hadith:

> Anas b. Malik reported that a person who had drink [sic] wine was brought to Allah's Apostle (may peace be upon him). He gave him forty stripes with two lashes. Abu Bakr also did that, but when Umar (assumed the responsibilities) of the Caliphate, he consulted people and Abd al-Rahman said: The mildest punishment (for drinking) is eighty (stripes) and 'Umar their [sic] prescribed this punishment.[7]

So the Islamic punishment for drinking alcohol—in any amount, large or small—is to be beaten with eighty lashes. In America, however, you are only punished for drinking alcohol if it causes you to do something that is dangerous to other people, like driving drunk.

Islamic law treats alcohol as something evil, but there is a big inconsistency within Islam about this subject. While alcohol is forbidden during a Muslim's life, it becomes one of the chief attractions of life after death in paradise!

In other words, if a good Muslim obeys sharia law and avoids drinking alcohol for his entire life, Allah will see the sacrifice this Muslim made and reward him with a river of alcohol in paradise. He won't get just a bottle of wine but a whole river created especially for him. Allah will also provide plenty of silver goblets spread around the edge of that river. And not just that: Allah will create unique servants who will look like little children to serve the alcohol in these goblets to the Muslim.

The Muslim will not even need to call the children to serve him. When the desire for alcohol comes to him, a child server will get a goblet, fill it from the river, and bring it to him. The children will be able to sense his desire and serve him. This is what we studied and learned in Quranic interpretation class at Al-Azhar. Here are the pertinent verses from the Quran:

> Verily, the *Abrâr* (pious, who fear Allah and avoid evil), shall drink a cup (of wine) mixed with water from a spring in Paradise called *Kâfûr*....And amongst them will be passed round vessels of silver and cups of crystal....And round about them will (serve) boys of everlasting youth. If you see them, you would think them scattered pearls.[8]

> —Surah 76:5, 15, 19, MUHSIN KHAN

Prohibiting alcohol in America

I was surprised to learn that there was a period in U.S. history when the federal government outlawed alcohol in the entire country (1920–1933). Of course, those who broke the law were not punished with eighty lashes, but they had to pay a fine or face jail time. That law lasted thirteen years before it was repealed. However, the Islamic prohibition of alcohol has been practiced for more than fourteen hundred years. No government can overrule this law. The change has to come from within the religion.

5. Stealing

Principle in conflict: cruel and unusual punishment

Many people have heard that someone caught stealing must have their right hand cut off, according to Islamic law. Americans can hardly comprehend this kind of cruelty. They wonder if it is just a radical interpretation of some obscure text. They at least assume that this kind of barbaric punishment would not be practiced today.

I am sorry to say that this punishment is clearly mandated in the Quran, and it is practiced today in countries where Islamic law is enforced. I saw it happen myself in Saudi Arabia. On the street one day I noticed hundreds of people gathering in a circle. When I looked closer, I saw that the police had just cut off a man's hand, and I saw his arm with the hand missing. The scene haunted me.

Here is what the Quran says:

> As to the thief, male or female, cut off his or her hands: a punishment by way of example, from Allah, for their crime: and Allah is Exalted in power.
>
> —Surah 5:38, ALI

What level of theft would merit such a harsh punishment? The Islamic law requires that if a person steals an amount equal to a quarter dinar (similar to a quarter dollar), his hand must be cut off:

> Aisha, second wife of Muhammad, said, "The prophet Muhammad said, the hand of the thief can be cut off for a quarter dinar or more."[9]

Most people don't realize that the punishment isn't complete after the hand is cut off. Islamic law says the severed hand must be hung around the criminal's neck on a rope and that the person must walk around the town so the people can see what happened even if they did not see the hand cut off:

> He said, "Cutting the hand off and hanging the hand around the neck of the person was sunnah (meaning it was done and practiced by the prophet himself).[10]

I think cutting off the hands is a particularly cruel punishment. It leaves no room for the criminal to repent and to be accepted back into society as a whole person. He will always be marked by what he did wrong in the past. To my knowledge, pre-Islamic Arabian society never had a law about cutting off the hands. This was one of the new laws Muhammad introduced.

Stealing in America

Believe it or not, I think the majority of ordinary Muslims would support Islamic law about stealing—even in America. They would think, "OK, the law will be enforced a few times and then no one will steal." They don't understand that if that law is enforced, no one will have two hands. The Enron executives who embezzled so much money from their company would have their hands cut off on national television.

6. Slander

Principle in conflict: cruel and unusual punishment

The basic punishment for slander, according to the Quran, is eighty lashes:

> And those who accuse honourable women but bring not four witnesses, scourge them (with) eighty stripes and never (afterward) accept their testimony—They indeed are evil-doers.
>
> —Surah 24:4, PICKTHAL

Slander has a unique position among the other great crimes in Islam, in that you can find mercy in the punishment for this crime, especially if you compare it to the punishment for adultery:

1. Slander must be confirmed by four witnesses—the same number of witnesses needed for the crime of

adultery (which is punished by being stoned to death).

2. The judge can reject some witnesses for slander, while none of the witnesses can be rejected for adultery.

3. The person accused of slander has the right to repent, and that repentance will cancel their sentence. Repentance will not change the punishment for adultery.[11]

To get a clear picture about the history of the crime of slander, you have to go to the time when the prophet of Islam lived and see how he practiced the law, and why.

The story starts with Muhammad's favorite wife, Aisha. Aisha accompanied Muhammad and his people on a raid. During the return trip, events occurred that made it look like Aisha committed adultery with a Muslim soldier.

Two witnesses testified against Aisha—Himnah bint Jahsh, who was the sister of one of Muhammad's other wives, and Hasan ibn Thabid, a man Muhammad loved for writing poetry that defended Islam against the idol worshipers and the Jews. Muhammad and the Muslim community were in turmoil for weeks as Muhammad contemplated how to deal with the situation.[12] Finally, he received a revelation, which is recorded in the Quran in Surah 24:11–20.

> Why did they not bring four witnesses of it? But as they have not brought witnesses they are liars before Allah.
> —Surah 24:13, SHAKIR

The revelation from the angel Gabriel established that Aisha was innocent of adultery because those who accused Aisha were "liars." This rescued Aisha from being stoned. But it also meant that Muhammad's poet and one of his sisters-in-law had committed slander and would need to take eighty lashes. So the revelation also provided a way of escape for them. It said:

> And those who accuse honourable women but bring not four witnesses, scourge them (with) eighty stripes.... Save those who afterward repent and make amends.
> —Surah 24:4–5, PICKTHAL

In other words, if a person slanders but then repents, he or she does not have to take the eighty lashes. Why do I discuss this point here? Because none of the Muslim scholars dare to think about how the revelations seem to rescue Muhammad from his problems. Islamic scholars turn off their critical thought processes because the Quran says:

> And whatsoever the Messenger (Muhammad) gives you, take it, and whatsoever he forbids you, abstain (from it), and fear Allâh. Verily, Allâh is Severe in punishment.
> —Surah 59:7, MUHSIN KHAN

If they try to use their logic or their minds to search for answers, they will cross the red line that was drawn by the prophet and they will be in a position of defiance against Allah and his prophet. They will be slapped in the face by another famous verse:

> O you who believe! do not put questions about things which if declared to you may trouble you.
> —Surah 5:101, SHAKIR

Slander in America

America has laws about slander, but none of them say that the sentence is to take eighty lashes. Again, this would violate the eighth amendment of the U.S. Constitution, which forbids cruel and unusual punishment.

An ordinary Muslim in an Islamic country has never heard that cruel and unusual punishment is bad. Instead, he sees that beating people up is a way of controlling them. Islamic governments commonly authorize torture and beatings in prison, and religious leaders use beatings to enforce sharia law. Physical abuse is a part of the Muslim's culture, and he has to live with it.

7. Murder

Principle in conflict: all men are created equal

Sharia law requires the punishment of murder to be death, and even the United States of America practices this punishment. In America, you will also see that the type of punishment for a murder is affected by the motivation and circumstances behind the murder. But in America today, you will not see a difference in punishment based on the type of victim—whether the victim was a man or woman, Muslim or non-Muslim, an old person or a young person. In America, every human being has equal value in the eyes of the law.

It wasn't always this way in America. There was a time in American history when the murder of a black man would be considered less than the murder of a white man. However, Americans have repented of their prejudice, and the law is written clearly now that every human life has equal worth.

However, sharia law does not put equal value on every life. The punishment for murder is described in Surah 2:178 (ALI):

> O ye who believe! the law of equality is prescribed to you in cases of murder: the free for the free, the slave for the slave, the woman for the woman. But if any remission is made by the brother of the slain, then grant any

reasonable demand, and compensate him with hand-some gratitude, this is a concession and a Mercy from your Lord. After this whoever exceeds the limits shall be in grave penalty.

Let's say a Muslim man kills a Christian. Under sharia law, this Muslim man will not be punished with the death penalty because a Christian life is worth less than a Muslim life. The great historian Ibn Kathir recorded Muhammad's position on this matter exactly:

> According to Ali ibn abu Talib, the apostle of Allah said a Muslim cannot be killed because he killed a Jew or an infidel.[13]

Also, Ibn Kathir said that the majority of Muslim scholars agree that a man cannot be killed for killing a woman because Surah 2:178 says equality means "woman for the woman."[14]

I think most ordinary Muslims today do not realize that Islamic law for murder puts different values on different human beings. They would probably be shocked to learn about it.

However, ordinary Muslims are well aware that many Islamic governments look the other way when a woman or girl is murdered for an honor killing. Jordan and other Arab Gulf countries have many honor killings. If a female's family discovers that she has sinned, she can disappear. The neighborhood will notice the woman is missing, but nobody will talk.

A personal memory

When I was in middle school in Egypt, I saw honor killings more than once. A couple of miles from my neighborhood was a huge irrigation canal coming off the Nile River. The canal was wide, and the water flowed swiftly. As a boy, my friends and I would go to the bridge over the canal and jump in the water to go swimming.

More than once I saw a man or a woman being shot and killed and thrown off the bridge into the canal. The body would sink down to the bottom of the river, but after a couple of days it would rise to the surface. Sometimes the water level was so high that the water reached the bottom of the bridge. So when a body reached the surface of the water and began to be pushed downstream, it would get caught against the bridge.

Sometimes we saw male corpses, but more often than not we saw female corpses. The body would stay stuck against the bridge for two or three days because no one would call the police. People in Egypt don't want to get near the police or be questioned because the police have a terrible reputation.

The worst honor killing I ever saw happened in the summertime when my friends and I were on the bridge preparing to jump in the water. On the other side of the canal was a road and then a cornfield. From out of the cornfield, we saw two men dragging a young girl in between them with her hands tied behind her back. They crossed the road and made her sit down and bend her head down toward the water. Then one man put a knife to her neck and decapitated her while the other man pushed her body into the water.

When I saw that, I screamed and screamed. It took weeks for me to recover. The first night I woke up in the middle of the night crying and screaming. I ran downstairs, flung open the front door, and ran into the street screaming. My family members ran after me, and I thought they were people trying to kill me, so I kept running and screaming. This was one of the most horrible things that happened in my childhood. I still wonder about this girl: for what crime was she killed?

Murder in America

America will never agree to go backward in human rights and civilization by allowing Islamic law to be practiced in the country. America will continue to move toward the ideal that was established at the birth of the nation, that "all men are created equal." A murderer will never be excused on the basis that his victim was a woman or a human being who practiced a different religion. In America, the law says that a person—man or woman, Muslim or not—is innocent until proven guilty beyond a shadow of a doubt.

Conclusion

Why is the Muslim world trapped in these seventh-century ideas of justice? It's because Islam is a religion and a way of life. Muhummad set up the system so that you cannot remove any part of it. The Quran says you cannot "believe in some and disbelieve in others" (Surah 4:150, Pickthal).

This is a very famous verse in the Muslim world, and the people understand what it means. You cannot accept the parts of Islam that you like and reject the parts that you don't like. You have to take it all. The Quran also says, "They can have no (real) Faith, until they make thee [Muhammad] judge in all disputes between them" (Surah 4:65, Ali).

This verse was revealed after some Muslims went to someone other than Muhammad to settle a dispute. The verse says that a Muslim has no faith unless he goes to Muhammad to judge all disputes. Radical Muslims always use this verse to say that if a Muslim rejects any part of Islamic law, then he has no faith or has left Islam. This makes it almost impossible for Islamic law to be modernized because the one who modifies the law is:

1. Not making Muhammad judge of all disputes
2. Proving he has no faith

To be a Muslim, you must obey Muhammad's words and example. The Quran says, "He who obeys the Messenger, obeys Allah" (Surah 4:80, ALI; see also Surah 4:64; 5:44; 5:49–50; 38:26).

The Quran makes it very hard for Muslims to reject the judgment of some of the crimes mentioned in this chapter while keeping the judgment of others. As I will discuss later in this book, the Muslim world needs a powerful reformation in how it reads and understands its books of history and law.

This kind of reformation can only come about in a free society that allows freedom of thought and religion. To get that kind of freedom, the Muslim world needs democracy. The next three chapters will explain what Islam teaches about democracy and how democracy can became a reality in the Middle East despite the current disaster in Iraq.

Fourteen
WHAT ISLAM TEACHES ABOUT DEMOCRACY

AT THE START OF THE TWENTY-FIRST CENTURY, THE UNITED States pursued the great dream of seeing democracy flourish in the Middle East. This was a new strategy for the United States. Before 9/11, the United States did not push to establish democracies. Instead, policy focused on keeping stability in the region. But the strategy changed after America led the defeat of the Taliban in Afghanistan and of Saddam Hussein and the Baath Party in Iraq. The new position of the United States was described simply by U.S. Secretary of State Condoleeza Rice during a speech at the American University in Cairo in 2005.

Rice told the people of the Middle East:

> We should all look to a future when every government respects the will of its citizens—because the ideal of democracy is universal. For 60 years, my country, the United States, pursued stability at the expense of democracy in this region here in the Middle East—and we achieved neither. Now, we are taking a different course. We are supporting the democratic aspirations of all people...
>
> We know these advances will not come easily, or all at once. We know that different societies will find forms of democracy that work for them. When we talk about democracy, though, we are referring to governments that protect certain basic rights for all their citizens—among

these, the right to speak freely. The right to associate. The right to worship as you wish. The freedom to educate your children—boys and girls. And freedom from the midnight knock of the secret police.

Securing these rights is the hope of every citizen, and the duty of every government.[1]

I fully agree with this strategy. The Muslim world needs democracy and freedom above all else. The ordinary, working-class Muslims are really the ones who suffer the most from the corrupt governments in Islam. They are the ones without jobs, basic services, security, and freedoms. They need a government to look after them and improve their lives. They need job opportunities, better education, health care, and help to open small businesses. Whichever government will provide these things for them is the government they want.

The uneducated are not sure which government would help them the most—a secular or a religious government. They are willing to try a democracy if it works. By the same token, they are willing to accept radical groups when they provide practical help for society, like schools and hospitals. They are looking for a government to serve them.

In practice, they do not want to live under Islamic law, but at the same time they want to be identified as an Islamic country that is based on the Quran. For example, in the first draft of the Iraqi constitution, you can see the love of Islam mixed with the desire for democracy. It says in section 1, article 2:

First: Islam is the official religion of the State and it is a fundamental source of legislation:
A. No law that contradicts the established provisions of Islam may be established.

B. No law that contradicts the principles of democracy may be established.[2]

While the people of Iraq want a democracy, they also want Islam as the official religion of the state. They do not want any law that "contradicts the established provisions of Islam."

It would be better to have separation of religion and state, as in America. But if you tried to leave out the part about Islam as the religion of the state, the people of Iraq would never accept this constitution.

Even the constitution of Egypt, which was established under Anwar Sadat, who was murdered by Islamic radicals for declaring separation of religion and state—even this constitution says that Islam is the state religion and that Islamic law is its principle source of legislation. Part 1, article 2 states:

> Islam is the Religion of the State. Arabic is its official language, and the principal source of legislation is Islamic Jurisprudence (Sharia).[3]

In short, ordinary Muslims identify themselves strongly with Islam, but they do not want to suffer for Islamic law and they would be happy to live under a democracy if it would improve their quality of life.

It is only the most liberal Muslims who call for a complete separation of religion and politics. These Muslims often have a Western education and believe that secular government is the best thing for the Muslim world. When America says her goal is to spread democracy, these are the only Muslims who really believe it.

If you want to know the deeper understanding of democracy in Islamic teaching, you don't talk to an ordinary Muslim. You go to the committed and the radical Muslims who study Islam deeply so they can apply it to their lives. Most radicals reject democracy completely, calling it an infidel, Western political system. However, many committed Muslims not only say that democracy is acceptable but also that it was practiced in the Muslim community long before it was practiced in the West.

Let's see how these two groups reach these conclusions.

Radicals Who Reject Democracy

Islamic radical movements all around the world totally reject democracy and say that democracy is not from Islam. To them, democracy is part of the infidel, Western political system. It has nothing to do with Allah or his prophet or the Quran.

This attitude was established by the leaders of modern Islamic radicalism—Hassan al-Bana (1906–1949), Abu-ala' Maududi (1903–1979), and Sayyid Qutb (1906–1965). A strong group of current Islamic scholars agree with them.[4]

This is how their logic takes its course.

1. Allah is the creator, and the right to rule belongs to him.

Dr. Mahmoud al-Kah'lidi, who was trained in law at Al-Azhar, wrote:

> In Islam, the rule belongs to Allah, and his laws, but in Western democracy, the rules belong to the people. And this cannot be reconciled with the Islamic principles of political system...We cannot see one single evidence in the Quran proving that the rule can be for the people, not for Allah. Every single verse in the Quran that speaks about this subject gives the authority to Allah and his laws. And the laws are those that were revealed to the prophet and they are not the ones that are passed by the Parliament or the Congress.[5]

It's easy to find verses in the Quran that talk about Allah having authority. Here are some examples:

> The command (or the judgment) is for none but Allâh.
> —Surah 12:40, MUHSIN KHAN

> He created the sun, the moon, and the stars, (all) governed by laws under His command. Is it not His to create and to govern?
> —Surah 7:54, ALI

> Allah…has no partner in (His) dominion.
> —Surah 17:111, ALI

> …nor does He share His Command with any person whatsoever.
> —Surah 18:26, ALI

> The things that my Lord has indeed forbidden are…joining partners (in worship) with Allâh for which He has given no authority.
> —Surah 7:33, MUHSIN KHAN

2. Democracy violates Islamic law because it steals the right to rule away from Allah and gives it to people.

From the radical point of view, any law that is not based on the teachings of Islam is an attack against Allah. Maududi, one of the founding fathers of modern Islamic terrorism, explained: "Though man is merely a weak slave to Allah, some men put the laws of Allah behind them and try to create new laws."[6]

The Quran says Allah will not tolerate man's making laws for himself. It is a lie against Allah.

> And say not concerning that which your tongues put forth falsely: "This is lawful and this is forbidden," so as

to invent lies against Allâh. Verily, those who invent lies against Allâh will never prosper.

—Surah 16:116, MUHSIN KHAN (see also Surah 7:3)

A person who follows man-made laws is nothing but a criminal and a transgressor of the law, says the Quran.

If any do fail to judge by (the light of) what Allah hath revealed, they are (no better than) Unbelievers.

—Surah 5:47, ALI

Radicals say Allah sent the Quran for the believers to use for their law:

Lo! We reveal unto thee the Scripture with the truth, that thou mayst judge between mankind by that which Allah showeth thee.

—Surah 4:105, PICKTHAL

3. Those who accept any political system that does not come from Islam have left the faith and will be rejected by Allah.

Radicals say that accepting democracy is like idol worship because it means a person is submitting to an authority other than Allah. To the radical, accepting democracy means choosing to leave Islam:

But no, by the Lord, *they can have no (real) Faith*, until they make thee judge in all disputes between them, and find in their souls no resistance against Thy decisions, but accept them with the fullest conviction.

—Surah 4:65, ALI, emphasis added

The bottom line of the radical position is that Allah established Islam as a faith and a way of life through Muhammad. No other source of religion or law will be accepted from the people. Democracy is a system that was not created by Allah; it was created in the minds of men. Any person who tries to rule by any law other than the law of Allah is saying that the laws of Allah are not good enough. That person is *kafir,* meaning "infidel."

If a leader does not follow Islamic law, then radicals believe that leader must be removed, because the Quran says:

> Obey not him whose heart We have made heedless of Our remembrance, who followeth his own lust and whose case hath been abandoned.
>
> —Surah 18:28, Pickthal

The radicals see democracy as a false government that Christians (Americans and Europeans) are trying to force upon them. If they bow to this pressure, they believe Allah will no longer protect or help them. They quote:

> And the Jews will not be pleased with you, nor the Christians until you follow their religion. Say: Surely Allah's guidance, that is the (true) guidance. And if you follow their desires after the knowledge that has come to you, you shall have no guardian from Allah, nor any helper.
>
> —Surah 2:120, Shakir

This verse says that Christians will not be pleased with Muslims unless Muslims convert to Christianity. If Muslims convert to Christianity, then Allah will no longer guide and help them. So Muslims see democracy as a Christian trap that will lead to their destruction because Allah will no longer protect them.

Committed Muslims Who Accept Democracy

The Muslim scholars who support democracy have a completely different understanding of democracy in Islamic history. Instead of saying that democracy has no place in Islam, they say that Islam practiced democracy in the beginning with no influence from non-Muslim sources.

They even say democracy wasn't originally established in the West but in Islam, hundreds of years before Europe or the West started to think about their form of democracy. This position is supported by a distinguished group of scholars.[7]

These scholars say that Islam calls for people to choose their representatives in the government, just as a democracy does. They say Islam gives people the right to make their leaders and representatives accountable to them, just as a democracy does. If a leader does wrong, the people can remove him from office.

These scholars accept the legitimacy of the different aspects of democracies, such as elections, the rule of the majority, the establishing of different political parties, the right of the minority, the freedom of the press, and an independent judicial system.

They say democracy is a way of practicing the Islamic principle of *al-shurra*, which was established by Muhammad himself. *Al-shurra* means to make decisions by consulting together. The Quran refers to this principle when it speaks of those "who (conduct) their affairs by mutual Consultation" (Surah 42:38, ALI). Islamic history shows the Muslim community made some decisions as a group.

Another verse in the Quran speaks of Muhammad consulting with the Muslims about the "conduct of affairs." Regarding the context of the verse, it appears that some Muslims had stayed behind from jihad against Muhammad's orders. Muhammad was lenient with them and asked Allah to forgive them. To show that they were accepted back into the Muslim community, Muhammad was to "consult with them upon the conduct of affairs" (Surah 3:159, PICKTHAL).

So these are verses from the Quran that some Islamic scholars will use to say that democracy was a part of the Islamic system during Muhammad's time.

The most well-known scholar supporting this position is Dr. Yusef Qaradawi, who is a household name in the Arabic-speaking world today because of his phone-in religious television program on Al-Jazeera and his Web site. He discusses democracy in his book *A Modern Islamic Legal Opinion*. In his book, Dr. Qaradawi responded to the following question from a Muslim in Algeria:

> I was shocked when I heard some Muslim radicals from Al-Jema'a Al-Islamiya [an Islamic radical group] say that democracy contradicts Islam. One of them brought a statement from a Muslim scholar saying that democracy is an infidel system because democracy is the rule of the people, but in Islam the rule has to be for Allah. Is this correct—that democracy is an enemy to Islam, and democracy is an infidel system?[8]

Dr. Qaradawi made five important points in his answer.

1. Islam gives people the right to choose who governs them.

Qaradawi said people have the right not to follow a leader they don't like. He was referring to a famous hadith where Muhammad said:

The best of your rulers are those whom you love and who love you, upon whom you invoke God's blessings and who invoke His blessing upon you. And the worst of your rulers are those whom you hate and who hate you, who curse you and whom you curse.[9]

2. Allah rejects the leader that the people don't like.

Muhammad said, "Three people's prayers will never reach above their heads...the first one is a leader the people don't like."

3. Allah rejects dictator regimes of the Muslim world for taking the position of God on Earth and taking the people of God for slaves.

Qaradawi compared dictators to the Egyptian pharaoh who declared, "No god do I know for you but myself" (Surah 28:38, ALI).

4. Democracy is a way for Muslims to reject dictators and to establish a leader who will treat them well.

Qaradawi explained:

> Believing in democracy or calling for democracy does not really mean you reject the right of Allah to be called governor. What we mean when we accept democracy is that we accept democracy as a sign of rejecting dictators and dictatorship.[10]

5. Muslims can adopt modern ideas and political systems, as long as they don't contradict the Quran.

This is a very important point. The radicals will not allow anything new into the Islamic system. If an idea wasn't a part of Muhammad's world, they won't accept it. Qaradawi allowed for more modernization. He wrote:

As I mentioned previously in some of my books, we Muslims have the right to adopt new ideas from others just under one condition: that these ideas do not contradict the Quran or Islamic law.[11]

Notice that Qaradawi set a limit to what ideas can be accepted, and that boundary is the Quran. So even though he will accept democracy, he would reject any human rights or freedoms that contradict Islam.

Mixing Government With Islam

Muslim scholars disagree about using democracy as a specific method of government, but they are in complete agreement about government in general. Their points of agreement are:

- The only one who has the right to lead is Allah.
- The Quran must be the constitution of Muslims. (See Surah 4:105.)
- The Holy Constitution (the Quran) must rule the Islamic world and ultimately the entire world. (See Surah 24:55.)
- The Quran must lead every part of human life, especially politics. Just as the U.S. Constitution defines American politics, the Quran must define Islamic politics.
- Law must originate with Allah, not with man. The only time a law can be established without a precedent in the Quran is when dealing with an issue that is not addressed in the Quran. For example, there is no precedent in Islamic history

for punishing traffic violations or for election procedures.

- Just as the U.S. Congress cannot pass a law in America that would contradict the U.S. Constitution, an Islamic government cannot pass a law that would contradict the Quran.

In other words, whether they accept democracy or not, the radical and committed Muslims will accept nothing less than an Islamic state whose laws are defined by the Quran and the hadith. If Islamic law restricts what other cultures believe to be human rights, such as freedom of religion, freedom of speech, and rights for women, then so be it.

Fifteen
ESTABLISHING DEMOCRACY IN IRAQ AND THE MIDDLE EAST

EVEN THOUGH MANY MUSLIMS ARE OPEN TO DEMOCRACY, some Muslim countries will be more difficult for establishing democracies than others. If you asked me which country in the Middle East, other than Iran, would be the most difficult place to establish a democracy, I would say Iraq.

In this chapter I will give you a simple explanation of why Iraq is causing such a problem for the world community. I will also explain how America can work to establish democracies in other Middle East countries—without military intervention—even before the problems in Iraq are solved.

Iraq's Shifting Sand

If you try to build a house, you don't build it on the sand because the foundation will keep sliding away. Iraq is dangerous ground for trying to establish democracy for three reasons:

1. The differences between the groups who live there
2. Its religious position in Islam
3. Its neighboring countries

Different people groups

The Iraqi people are not like the people in other Arab countries that have mainly one belief and one language. Iraq is divided into three major groups—Shiites, Sunni Arabs, and Sunni Kurds—with different languages.

- The Shiites (or Shia), who make up the majority, are most closely related to the people of Iran, not to the Arabs. They mainly speak Arabic, and a few speak Farsi, or Persian. (Persian is the main language of Iran.) The Shiites are in the south and center of the country, and in Baghdad.

- The Sunni Arabs are in the minority, but they held the power under Saddam's dictatorship. They speak Arabic. The Sunnis are in western Baghdad and have a small presence in the north where the Kurds are the majority.

- The Kurdish people are related to other Kurds who are spread between Syria and Turkey and Iran, and they speak Kurdish. Though they are Sunni Muslim, they do not relate to the Sunni Arabs of Iraq. The Kurds are mostly in the north.

These separate groups don't provide a solid foundation to establish a new government that will work together. It would be much easier with one people, one language, and one religion.

The problem right now in Iraq is religious, not political. The Sunnis and Shiites are in a depressing cycle of attack and retaliation.

Many people talk about how the Sunnis and Shiites got along before the fall of Saddam, but now they are killing each other. What caused the change? I will explain.

During the dictatorship of Saddam Hussein, the Shia organized a radical group called Hizb-at-Dawa to fight against him. Most of the leaders of this group went into exile outside of Iraq before America defeated Saddam Hussein.

After Saddam fell, some of these Shiite radicals returned to Iraq and seem to have merged with Moqtada al-Sadr and his

Al-Mahdi army. They started causing trouble to the Sunnis. At the same time, the top leaders of Hizb-at-Dawa became active in the new government. The former leader of the group (Ibrahim Jafeeri) was the second prime minister of Iraq, and the former second-in-command of the group (Nori al-Maliki) is now the third prime minister of Iraq.

Here's why the situation has escalated in a way that it didn't during Saddam's time. Under Saddam, the Sunnis did not have a radical group in Iraq. Instead, the Sunnis' interests were represented by the secular Baath Party. After Saddam fell, former members of the Baath Party united with a new radical Sunni group that is supported by Al-Qaeda. In addition, Muslim Sunni radicals are coming in from other countries to fight with them. Radical groups have been very successful at attracting followers in Iraq because they have been able to frame the battle as a fight between Islam and Christianity.

In short, a civil war is breaking out between Shiites and Sunnis because the government of Iraq is run by former leaders of the Shiite radical group and the Sunnis are upset. The fighting is about religion and retaliation, not politics anymore. The death squads come from both sects.

There is one area of Iraq that is somewhat spared this bloodshed—the north. Kurds make up the majority in northern Iraq, and they are not causing trouble. The problems in the north are only caused by the small group of Sunnis that lives in that area.

The religious position of Baghdad

I don't know how much America understands the historical and religious position of Baghdad and Iraq in the heart of Muslim people. Baghdad is one of the five historical capitals of Islam, among which are Cairo, Medina, Damascus, Baghdad, and Jerusalem. The fall of Baghdad reminded the people in the Middle East of the fall of the Islamic caliphate in Turkey in 1924, which was a seismic event.

In the eyes of the Muslim world, Baghdad and Iraq are now occupied by what Muslims consider to be a Christian country (America), which is supported by another Christian country (Great Britain). To them, it looks like a new round of Western crusades against the Islamic world. (It didn't help when President George W. Bush made the semantic blunder of declaring a "crusade" against terrorism shortly after 9/11.)

This situation makes it easy for radical groups to recruit members to fight for the sake of Islam. Islamic radicals from all over the Muslim world are sneaking into Iraq and joining the insurgence against the American military. They are different types of people with different motivations, but for the moment they also fight for a common cause—to get the "infidel," America, out of their country.

Iraq's neighbors

Iraq is a landlocked country bordered by six different nations. The most dangerous countries are Syria to the west and Iran to the east. But Turkey, Saudi Arabia, and Jordan are also troubling countries. The only benign country is Kuwait.

Ammunitions and fighters slip across the borders of Syria, Iran, Jordan, and Saudi Arabia to fight in Iraq. Turkey has a sensitive position because Turkish people are living on the border between Turkey and Iraq.

America Needs to Stay

Even though it is a rough place to establish democracy, America should not give up in Iraq. America needs to put Iraq's situation under control. Train more Iraqi troops. Encourage the Iraqi government to be more involved in controlling the country. Keep working on diplomacy between the Sunnis, Shiites, and Kurds. Get them to agree to lead the country together and take care of it. If America cannot succeed with diplomatic efforts to bring these three groups together, America is not going to get them to agree with military power.

America also needs to deal with the radicals. Most of them will reject democracy completely, so they will not come to the negotiating table to work out a political solution. If the radicals fought against the American military directly, the United States would have no problem defeating them. Instead, their strategy has been to create terror in society in general, disrupting the ability of the government to establish stability and security and work out diplomatic solutions between the different people groups.

A lot of people wonder why radical groups will set off a bomb in a crowded market or parking lot, where most of the victims will be other Muslims. After all, the Quran clearly condemns Muslims killing other Muslims.

> O you who believe...do not kill your people.
> —Surah 4:29, SHAKIR

The radicals apply a scary logic to justify terrorism in Iraq. In their eyes, most of the civilians, the national police force, and the national military accept democracy and are cooperating with infidel invaders (the United States and her allies). Anyone who does this has betrayed Islam and is no longer a Muslim. Since these people are no longer Muslims and they are cooperating with the enemy, they *are* the enemy. The Quran tells Muslims to fight anyone who is fighting against Islam.

From the radical point of view, fighting is not only justified, but it is also an obligation. These extreme radicals do not accept the option of winning people's hearts by building schools or creating jobs. Even though the way of peace may be a more effective strategy for gaining political power, they won't consider it. If they tried to improve a democratic society, it would mean they were cooperating with the infidels and accepting their infidel government.

The radicals use a strategy of fear. This was also Muhammad's strategy when he battled unbelievers. The Quran says:

> Soon shall We cast terror into the hearts of the Unbelievers.
>
> —Surah 3:151, ALI

> Remember thy Lord inspired the angels (with the message): "I am with you: give firmness to the Believers: I will instill terror into the hearts of the Unbelievers."
>
> —Surah 8:12, ALI

> Against them make ready your strength to the utmost of your power, including steeds of war, to strike terror into (the hearts of) the enemies.
>
> —Surah 8:60, ALI

Radicals want to put fear in the heart of the majority and then take over the government by force. They say, "If you resist us taking over the government by force, then you will suffer." Their goal is to establish an Islamic government with Islamic law.

If the American military leave Iraq alone too soon, I believe the Shiite militants, like Moqtada al-Sadr, will take over by force. The Sunnis will not welcome that, and it will be the beginning of a horrible, long-term religious civil war. Iraq would be destroyed by it. It would take decades to recover. It would be much worse than the civil war in Lebanon, which lasted twenty years.

The reason I believe the government will fall to Shiite radicals is because Iran, which borders Iraq, is watching for an opportunity to exert more influence in Iraq. When America leaves Iraq, Iran will not sit and watch. It will support the Shiite militants, and Iraq will become a radical country like Iran. I believe the Iranian regime is pushing America to withdraw because they are already planning for this.

I don't believe Iraq will fall to the Sunni radicals. The Sunni militants in Iran will never be as powerful as the Shiite militants because they don't have a powerful nation nearby that will support them.

Other Places for Democracy

Though America can't walk away from Iraq right now, America can start now to establish democracy in other Middle East nations. There are places where the United States has a good chance of success with less effort than in Iraq.

America needs to search for a country that doesn't have different competing groups who speak different languages, have different beliefs, and promote different interests. America needs a country that is not bordered by too many different countries, whether they are fanatic or not. Why not pick a country like Egypt or Libya?

Democracy in Egypt

Egypt is bordered by sea on the north and east, by Sudan from the south, and by Libya from the west. Egypt's neighbors would not affect the establishment of democracy.

Egypt has only two different people groups—Muslims and Christians. Christians will be the first group to welcome and support democracy. In addition, the majority of Muslims are secular, mostly liberal, and will have no fear of democracy.

The only challenge America would face in Egypt is a small pocket of Islamic radicalism. And this pocket does not require 150,000 U.S. soldiers to invade the country to deal with them. The Egyptian government has kept them under control for many years.

The United States already helps Egypt with about $1 to $2 billion in aid every year since 1979.[1] All the United States needs to do is tell President Mubarek, "Sir, we would like to increase U.S. aid to your country. We would like to help your government and your economy, and we ask only one favor: we would like you to establish a real democracy in your country. We will stand behind you so you will succeed."

Egypt is considered to be the capital of the Arab world. The success of democracy in Egypt would spread all over the Middle East without one single bullet. It would be like throwing a stone in the water, and the ripples would spread everywhere.

Democracy in Libya

A country like Libya is another good opportunity for democracy. Libya is comprised of almost all Arabs, except for a tiny group in the western part of the country called Barbars and another tiny group in the south that are descendants of Saharan Africans. These little groups are not big enough to cause conflict.

Libya is controlled by a vicious dictator, Muammar al-Qaddafi, but he is sensitive to America's attitude toward him. After the U.S. invasion of Iraq, Qaddafi declared that he was giving up his nuclear weapons program and resolving his problem with the West, especially Europe, Britain, and the

United States. America took Libya's name off the terrorist list, started normalizing political relations, and opened embassies in Tripoli, the capital of Libya.

However, Qaddafi's openness to diplomatic persuasion may fade away if the West doesn't become more involved with him. Qaddafi expected a greater reward for giving up his nuclear program than what he received. Then he saw Iran defy the world and continue its nuclear weapons program, and I think he was even more disappointed that he surrendered his own. So he started complaining publicly that America and Europe did not keep their promises to him.

Europe, America, and England need to start wooing Qaddafi, inviting him to visit their countries and developing a positive relationship with him. They need to understand his personality and mind-set. When he was a young man, he led a military coup and has been Libya's top leader from that time until now—more than thirty years. He has been without guidance all this time, like riding a horse with no reins. Fifteen years ago, he wrote the "green book," which set out to establish a new political system in his country. It was a mixture of open market, communism, dictatorship, and modernism. No human being in Libya could raise a hand to discuss it because Qaddafi would cut off that hand.

However, I believe Qaddafi might choose to listen to outside sources that could teach him about different political systems. If he has a good plan and a good incentive, I believe he would establish democracy in his country, and he would not need a single American soldier to do it.

Libya's borders will not create too much of a threat for establishing democracy. The country is bordered by Egypt to the east and the Mediterranean Sea to the north. To the south are

Niger, Chad, and Sudan; to the west are Tunisia and Algeria. The greatest potential for trouble would be the border with Algeria because of fighting between radicals and the secular government of Algeria. But Qaddafi has proved in the past that he is capable of securing his borders. Radicals have targeted his regime for many years, but he remains in control.

Conclusion

Iraq is a hard place to start a democracy because of the differences between the groups who live there, its religious position in Islam, and its neighboring countries. While the United States continues efforts there, it should also move forward to encourage democracy in more receptive countries in the Middle East, like Egypt and Libya.

Sixteen
SEPARATING RELIGION AND POLITICS

WHILE THE UNITED STATES IS BUSY ENCOURAGING democracy in the Muslim world, it needs to be aware that democracy alone will not produce freedom and human rights. Democracy alone will not separate religion and politics. You can see this easily by looking at the country of Iran.

Both the United States and Iran are republics, meaning, according to Webster's, "the supreme power is held by the citizens entitled to vote and is exercised by elected officers and representatives governing according to law." However, Iran operates its republic in an Islamic way that Americans would never recognize as a democratic system like their own.

You will often hear radicals in Muslim countries demand to have the Quran as their constitution. If you've ever read the Quran, you will wonder how a government could operate based on it. The nation of Iran is the best example in the world today of a nation that has based its political system on the Quran as a constitution. Now we will examine the Iranian constitution and get a practical view of how a government under Islam functions.

The Constitution of Iran

If you read the entire constitution of Iran (which you can easily do on the Internet), you will recognize the same elements of a republic that operate in the United States—for example, a congress and president elected by the people, guarantees of rights for different groups, and a system of courts.

However, you will also see that all these functions are explicitly restricted by the teachings of Islam. Article 1 of the constitution eliminates any doubt about whether there is a separation of religion and politics:

> The form of government of Iran is that of an Islamic Republic, endorsed by the people of Iran on the basis of their long-standing belief in the sovereignty of truth and Quranic justice.[1]

Religion and politics are inseparably fused together in Iran. This mind-set carries over into the way government members are elected. For example, the constitution establishes an Islamic Consultative Assembly, which has 270 elected members. However, the constitution states specifically how many non-Muslims can be represented in the assembly. So, out of 270 members, the Zoroastrians and Jews choose one, the Chaldean Christians choose one, and the Armenian Christians in the north choose one.[2] Out of 270 representatives, the non-Muslim point of view is represented by three people.

These three non-Muslims will have a hard time affecting legislation. For example, new bills must be sponsored by fifteen members of the Islamic Consultative Assembly in order to be introduced.[3] Since non-Muslims only have three representatives, there is little chance that they can introduce any bills to the assembly. In an Islamic republic, having elections does not guarantee fair representation.

Although the Islamic Consultative Assembly can draft laws, the laws must be approved by twelve experts in Islamic law, called the Guardian Council. Six of these men are appointed by the leader (president), and six are elected by the Islamic Consultative Assembly from among the Muslim jurists nominated by the head of the judicial power.[4] The job of the Guardian Council is to protect Allah's exclusive right to create law[5] by ensuring that no law goes against Islamic principles. The constitution states:

> All legislation passed by the Islamic Consultative Assembly must be sent to the Guardian Council. The Guardian Council will review it within a maximum of ten days from its receipt with a view to ensuring it compatibility with the criteria of Islam and the Constitution. If it finds the legislation incompatible, it will return it to the Assembly for review. Otherwise the legislation will be deemed enforceable.[6]

In conclusion, the Islamic-style republic restricts the power of the people to govern in several ways:

1. Allah must be recognized as the one who ultimately holds all political authority. Religion and politics are bound together.
2. The power of the people to govern themselves is restricted to following the teachings of Islam.
3. Non-Muslims are not permitted to have enough power in the government to affect the law.

The goal of an Islamic government is to protect and promote Islam in every way possible.

The American Republic

The U.S. Constitution also establishes a republic but without the religious restrictions. In other words, when the people in each state vote for a member of the House of Representatives or the Senate, they are not required to make a certain decision based on the faith of the person. The president does not need to be Christian, for example, although many Muslims overseas will assume the U.S. president is a Christian and speaks for all the Christians in the United States. That's because their leaders are Muslim and speak from the Muslim point of view.

The American-style republic differs from the Islamic-style republic because:

1. The citizens, not God, function as the supreme power of the political system.
2. The laws created by the citizens are not restricted according to any religious belief.
3. Religious persuasion does not restrict the ability of a person to run for office.

Many of the founders of America left Europe in order to find a place where they could practice religion as they desired. Under these circumstances, it might have been natural to establish their beliefs as the official religion of the States. Instead, they chose to protect their religious freedom by establishing no state religion at all.

Conclusion

I believe the ultimate goal in the Middle East needs to be the separation of religion and politics. This isn't going to happen in one step. The ordinary Muslims would never tolerate it. But in the future I hope they will see that when they separate religion and politics, they will be able to practice Islam with more freedom. They will be able to allow Islam to grow into the twenty-first century.

SECTION V

THE FUTURE OF
THE CULTURE CLASH

Seventeen
FIFTY YEARS FROM NOW

I HAVE BEEN ASKED, "WHAT WILL THE RELATIONSHIP BETWEEN the Muslim world and the rest of the world look like in fifty years?"

The answer depends on who will rule in the Islamic world and influence society—secular Muslims, radicals, or dictators?

In the next fifty years, I don't think dictator regimes will be able to keep power. One of the keys to a dictatorship keeping power is the control of information. Twenty or thirty years ago, a dictator could control access to all the information the people in his country received. Today that is quickly becoming impossible.

Unfortunately, I fear that secular Muslims will also be unable to hold on to power. By the end of the next fifty years, America may not be the supreme power of the world. Another power will compete with America—like China, Russia, or the European Union—and this power is not going to take the hard line against terrorists that America does. Radical groups will have the opportunity to strengthen and take control of national governments. Radicals will be the ones in charge if secular Muslims fail to lead.

World War III?

It could take less than fifty years for the world to face a crisis from Islamic radicals. In the next twenty years, Iran could get nuclear weapons and Pakistan could be ruled by radicals. In this case, a world war could happen easily. All it would take is for one of them to hit Israel with a nuclear weapon. If Israel can't respond, then America will defend Israel, possibly with nuclear capabilities. This will easily lead the world into World War III.

What if Muslim nations with nuclear weapons found a way to attack America directly? It would be like Al-Qaeda hitting America with nuclear or biological weapons on 9/11 instead of just airplanes. How would America respond? I think America would drop its own nuclear weapons on whatever place attacked them.

The best way to avoid this scenario is to separate religion from politics in the Muslim world. This needs to be deeper than just changing the words of the constitutions. This change must occur in the Muslim psyche and in the theology and teaching of Islam.

In other words, separation of religion and politics must happen in government, but it must also happen in the hearts of the Muslim people. Even if the whole Islamic world is ruled by secular governments, if the teaching of Islam still combines religion and politics, there will still be a problem. The Muslim people will stand on the teachings of Islam to rebel against the secular governments. The anger against the secular government will just create many underground Muslim radical groups to fight for overthrowing the secular regime and applying Islamic law.

Reformation of Islam

It will take two steps to separate politics and religion in the Muslim world. First, there has to be a new theology established, and second, this new theology needs to be communicated to the people in an acceptable way.

Establishing new theology

The new theology will require a new way of interpreting all of the Quran and hadith. Separating religion and politics will mean having a completely new perspective on all of the teachings.

It is my hope that Muslims in America and the West would work with Muslim scholars in the Islamic world to develop this new interpretation of the Quran. They can start by dealing with the verses and chapters that encourage Muslims to do jihad. If you read the Quran cover to cover, you will find that 60 percent of it is related to the holy wars (jihad) that were led by Muhammad and his followers.[1] You can't pretend those verses aren't there, as some liberals try to do. You have to acknowledge them and establish their meaning for the twenty-first century.

Modern scholars could say, for example, that jihad was necessary in the beginning of Islam because the new believers were persecuted and needed to protect themselves. But now there are more than 1.3 billion Muslims in the world. Muslims are powerful enough to survive, so now there is no need to practice jihad. Jihad for today should look to the example of the Islamic Sufi movement from the 1200s and 1300s. While acknowledging the existence of physical jihad in the past, they could say jihad for today is a personal, spiritual struggle to be holy in their relationship with God and others.

The Muslim world also needs a way to openly discuss the teachings of Islam. Muslims have been programmed to submit to Allah and his prophet without question. If anyone in the Muslim community asks questions about Islam, the rest of the community condemns and silences him. The Muslim media are not safe places for discussion. So the world community needs to provide a safe platform for Muslims to discuss new ways of interpreting the Quran and hadith.

Communicating the new theology

Even after a theology is established, the real problem will be communicating it to the Muslim people and having them agree with it. It will take the right people to preach this new interpretation of the Quran. If the liberals try to do this, they will be rejected by committed Muslims and by ordinary Muslims who don't respect the liberals anyway. The leadership has to come from committed Muslims, who have the respect of the ordinary Muslims. If people like Yusef Qaradawi, the popular imam with a show on the Al-Jazeera television network, would lead the movement, it would work. However, there is no sign that he or anyone at his level would be willing to do this.

Securing the Future

The best political strategy in the Muslim world is for America and her allies to establish and support as many successful, democratic governments as possible. The challenge is to make sure the people don't vote in radical leaders who will take away human rights and freedoms by following Islamic law. The hope is that freedom of thought in the Muslim world will allow Muslims to establish a new theology and teaching that will separate religion and politics.

Fifty years from now, if secular, liberal Muslims have power, the relationship between Muslim nations and the rest of the world will be much better.

Eighteen
THE WAR OF IDEAS

Stability, peace, and prosperity in the Muslim world depend on Muslims accepting the separation of politics and religion. This battle isn't fought with tanks and guns. It is a war of ideas and information that is fought through the media of the Muslim world and the media of the Western world. On both fronts there are half-truths and false information that plague the world media. It's important to be knowledgeable of both.

The Muslim World

The Muslim world needs to see how the Islamic way of life compares to the way of life in the rest of the world. They need to ask why most of the world has been able to reach some type of peace and stability, especially in Europe and the New World (meaning America, Canada, Australia, New Zealand, and South America) while the Muslim world has not. It's because the rest of the world has separated religion from politics.

The media in the Muslim world need to bring an honest picture of how the rest of the world functions, what it believes, and its ways of life. Instead, the Muslim media are full of lies and propaganda. There is no freedom of information. Instead, those with power try to control the people by controlling their information.

To fight the war of ideas in the Muslim world, you have to look at how their media channels operate. Let's look at the different types of media and the lies they present to the people.

Government-sponsored media

You can mainly find two types of media in the Muslim world—government-sponsored or radical.

Government-sponsored media include the influential television stations Al-Jazeera from Qatar (one of the six Arab Gulf countries) and Al-Arabiyya from Saudi Arabia. Other important national television stations are the LBC (the Lebanese National Broadcast) and Nile Broadcast (the Egyptian broadcast station). Every country has its own newspapers and magazines, too.

The Arabic media have no understanding of defending the interests of the public or creating a balance between the public and the government. This mentality was born and raised in the midst of dictator politics and Islamic fascism. The media will do everything asked of them by the dictator regimes.

The motivation of government-sponsored media is usually nationalism and supporting the regime in each country. For example, in a dictator country the media work hard to make the dictator appear to be a hero.

The government media create a bad picture of America specifically and of the West in general. They will never acknowledge the good things America has done for Arabs and Muslims. For example, this media failed to report how NATO and America used their military to rescue Muslims in Yugoslavia from Slobodan Milosevic, the Serbian leader.

While Muslims were crying for their people in Yugoslavia, their media never told them that Saddam Hussein, the dictator of Iraq, had a very close relationship with Milosevic, the one killing the Muslims. Saddam Hussein was always lifted up by most of the media in the Middle East as the one defending Arabs and Muslims because of his connection to the family of Muhammad.

In addition, America supported the *mujadin* in Afghanistan against the Soviet occupation. Because of America's help, this *mujadin* forced the Soviets to leave the country. The Islamic media don't want to report that, either.

When Muslims were hit by the tsunami in Asia, the United States and other Western countries sent aid. However, the Arab Gulf countries did not release their oil money to help their brothers, the Muslims in Indonesia and other countries in Asia. Muslims need to know this.

The bottom line is that the Muslim world gets an absolutely warped picture of world events. Their opinions and attitudes about the West are based on incomplete information.

Radical Muslim media

Radicals have their own media outlets to influence the Muslim world. There are magazines, newspapers, and Internet Web sites. The TV station Al-Minar in Lebanon is run by Hezbollah, a violent radical group. The Internet is being exploited especially well by Al-Qaeda, recruiting radicals around the world.

Even Islamic media that are not *controlled* by radicals are willing to *cooperate* with radicals. After 9/11, Al-Jazeera TV became like the channel of Al-Qaeda and other Muslim radicals. It presented radical voices and sympathized with them. Al-Jazeera accepted videotapes from Al-Qaeda leaders like Osama bin Laden or Ayman Zawahiri and broadcast them to the world. (Al-Arribiya TV did the same.)

One of Al-Jazeera's correspondents, Tayseer Alouni in Afghanistan, was the only journalist able to interview bin Laden after 9/11. He was later arrested for collaborating with Al-Qaeda and was tried in Spain, where he holds citizenship. He was sentenced to seven years in prison.[1]

Fixing America's image

Because of this false presentation in the media, America and the West must fix their image in the Muslim world. One way to do this is to establish any type of fair media that may encourage other Middle Eastern media to present a fair picture. I don't say America has to pay for this media so it will work for America. No, but I say America needs to encourage the government media to be fair in dealing with the issues and these problems.

For example, America is giving Egypt aid every year. America has the right to ask Egypt to use some of the money to improve training for the media. A program like this could be called the American Egyptian Media Association. This would be a way of helping the country to develop. America can't keep spending $1 to $2 billion every year to feed Egyptians while the media continue to poison them.

The media in the West also need to expose how the Muslim media are poisoning the Muslim world. For example, the media in the West can start reporting the false information and the weak information that is presented in the Muslim media.

The Non-Muslim World

The second front in the war of ideas is the non-Muslim world. The people of the non-Muslim world have an imaginary picture in their minds about Islam. It is a nice religion, and Muhammad was nice, just like Jesus. They think Muslims are very spiritual and peaceful people because they pray so much and fast for an entire month. Non-Muslims absolutely need to be exposed to the reality about the teachings of Islam.

The goal of all my writings is to take away that imaginary picture and replace it with the actual picture. As long as the West imagines Islam to be a peaceful religion, it will be passive about the danger. I feel obligated to warn America and the West that the threat is real.

Islam is not just another religion like the other religions of the world that will never threaten America. The problem is not just some crazy radical groups. The problem is not a specific, individual political regime. The problem is a fourteen-hundred-year-old religion and culture. The problem won't respond to a short response in a short time; it needs a great response over the long term.

I want to support moderate and liberal Muslims as human beings. But here's what bothers me. Many of them will present a picture of Islam to the West that is peaceful and loving. They quote all the nicest passages from the Quran and the hadith. But they don't explain that the Quran and hadith are not characterized by these nice sayings.

If you had a scale and you put all the Quran's nice sayings on one side and all the teachings about jihad and Islamic law on the other side, the nice side would hit the ceiling and the jihad side would be on the floor. Moderates and liberals need to explain how the teaching about jihad and Islamic law can be reinterpreted.

The West needs to recognize the real issues in Islamic theology and support the Muslim community in coming up with a new interpretation for this material.

Epilogue
RESOLVING THE CULTURE CLASH

HERE'S THE BOTTOM LINE OF THIS BOOK: THE WAR TODAY is between seventh-century Islamic culture and twenty-first-century modern culture. These cultures are incompatible. They cannot coexist because the values of one violate the values of the other.

In this book, I gave you a picture of seventh-century Islamic culture as it was articulated by Muhammad and lived out in Arabia. I also told you how this teaching has been passed down through the centuries and continues to rule the Muslim world today. In fact, this culture has changed very little in the fourteen hundred years since it began. When different groups of Muslims have tried to modernize, radicals and fundamentalists have pulled them back to the seventh century. So when you look at Islamic culture, remember: it *is* because it *was*.

Because this book gave you a picture of seventh-century Islamic culture, please don't use this picture to stereotype individual Muslims. Every individual is different, and each one deserves to be evaluated by his own actions. The purpose of this picture is to give you an understanding of the way Islamic society functions as a whole.

There is only one way to resolve the clash between seventh-century Islamic culture and the twenty-first century: Islamic culture has to change. The only way for Islamic culture to change is to have a new interpretation of the Quran and the hadith.

Some liberal Muslims want to pretend that human rights were recognized in the seventh century or that jihad was mostly an inner struggle. This is a fake picture of the past.

This strategy only works on the Westerners because ordinary Muslims will know better.

Change can only come through Muslim leaders who acknowledge the facts about the origins of Islam. These Muslim leaders need to interpret the facts in a way that fits with the new circumstances of modern society. As this happens, the Muslim world can begin to separate religion and politics and establish democracies with freedom of religion and speech. This will take the Muslim culture out of conflict with the modern world, and then Muslim culture can become a blessing to the world community instead of a curse.

Notes

Preface

1. Eve Conant, "A Bombthrower's Life," *Newsweek*, February 26, 2007, http://www.msnbc.msn.com/id/17201010/site/ newsweek/ (accessed May 22, 2007). Ali currently works at a conservative think tank in the United States, protected by armed bodyguards paid for by the Dutch government.

2. The CIA World Factbook, "Egypt," https://www.cia.gov/ library/publications/the-world-factbook/print/eg.html (accessed June 4, 2007).

2 — The Past Rules the Present

1. The rest of Surah 5:82 declares that "nearest among them in love to the believers wilt thou find those who say, 'We are Christians': because amongst these are men devoted to learning and men who have renounced the world, and they are not arrogant." This is a good endorsement of Christians, but it doesn't hold up against the other verses that condemn the Christian faith. (See Surah 5:18; 9:30.)

4 — Fasting and Pilgrimage

1. See *Sahih Bukhari*, vol. 1, bk. 6, no. 301, narrated by Abu Said al-Khudri, http://www.usc.edu/dept/MSA/fundamentals/ hadithsunnah/bukhari/006.sbt.html (accessed June 11, 2007). All references to *Sahih Bukhari* are translated by M. Muhsin Khan and are available through the USC-MSA Compendium of Muslim Texts at http://www.usc. edu/dept/MSA/fundamentals/hadithsunnah/bukhari/.

2. My teachers at Al-Azhar Middle School taught this story to students in class. You can find variations of it in the different books of Islamic history.

3. Ibn Kathir, *The Quran Commentary*, vol. 1, pt. 2 (Mansura, Egypt: Faith Library, 1996), p. 48–49.

4. *Sahih Muslim*, bk. 7, no. 3151, http://www.usc.edu/ dept/MSA/fundamentals/hadithsunnah/muslim/007. smt.html (accessed June 11, 2007). All references to *Sahih Muslim* are translated by Abdul Hamid Siddiqui and are available through the USC-MSA Compendium of Muslim Texts at http://www.usc. edu/dept/MSA/fundamentals/hadithsunnah/muslim/.

5 — Daily Life

1. These dates were obtained by looking at the Surah commentary by Syed Abu-Ala' Maududi available through the USC-MSA Compendium of Muslim Texts at http://www. usc.edu/dept/MSA/quran/maududi/mau4.html and http:// www.usc.edu/dept/MSA/quran/maududi/mau5.html (accessed May 19, 2007). The University of Southern California Web site makes it easy to look at Maududi's commentary on specific chapters of the Quran.

2. *Malik's Muwatta,* bk. 42, no. 42.5.13, http://www.usc. edu/dept/MSA/fundamentals/hadithsunnah/muwatta/042. mmt.html (accessed June 11, 2007). All references to *Malik's Muwatta* are translated by 'A'isha 'Abdarahman at-Tarjumana and Ya'qub Johnson and are available through the USC-MSA Compendium of Muslim Texts at http://www.usc. edu/dept/MSA/fundamentals/hadithsunnah/muwatta/.

3. I sometimes have people complain that I distort the Quran by only quoting part of a verse or a passage. I do this to make it easier for the reader who tends to get bogged down in too much wordiness. But for the record, here is the rest of the passage about usury: "But if ye turn back, ye shall have your capital sums: Deal not unjustly, and ye shall not be dealt with unjustly. If the debtor is in a difficulty, grant

him time till it is easy for him to repay. But if ye remit it by way of charity, that is best for you if ye only knew" (Surah 2:279–280, ALI). This basically says that Allah will forgive this group of people for charging interest if they treat the debtors with kindness, such as giving them extra time to pay. This sounds nice for the debtor, but the point I am trying to make is that this kindness was obligated upon the lenders by the threat of war.

4. Abdul Salam Faraj, "Today's Rulers Are in a Retreat Away From Islam," in *The Abandoned Duty*, quoted in Rifaat Sayed Ahmed, *The Armed Prophet* (London: Riad El-Rayyes Books, 1991, in Arabic).

5. See Surah 33:37–38; Ibn Kathir, *The Quran Commentary*, vol. 3, pt. 6, p. 239; *Sahih Bukhari*, vol. 9, bk. 93, no. 516, narrated by Anas, http://www.usc.edu/dept/MSA/fundamentals/hadithsunnah/bukhari/093.sbt.html (accessed June 11, 2007).

6 — Stereotypes About Non-Muslims

1. The USC-MSA Compendium of Muslim Texts defines *kafir* as "a person who refuses to submit himself to Allah (God), a disbeliever in God," while *kufr*, a similar spelling and definition, means "to show ungratefulness to Allah and not to believe in Him and His religion." See http://www.usc.edu/dept/MSA/reference/glossary/term.KAFIR.html and http://www.usc.edu/dept/MSA/reference/glossary/term.KUFR.html (accessed June 11, 2007).

7 — The Wall Between Muslims and Non-Muslims

1. The full text of this book, *Milestones Along the Road*, is available online at http://majalla.org/books/2005/qutb-nilestone.pdf (accessed June 11, 2007).

9 — Muhammad's Stereotypes About Women

1. Ibn Kathir, *The Quran Commentary*, as quoted in Ahmed To'fa'ha, *Women and Islam* (Beiruit, Lebanon, 1985), 36.

2. Ahmed To'fa'ha, *Women and Islam*, 33.

3. *Sahih Bukhari*, vol. 1, bk. 6, no. 301, narrated by Abu Said al-Khudri, http://www.usc.edu/dept/MSA/fundamentals/ hadithsunnah/bukhari/006.sbt.html (accessed June 11, 2007).

4. Al-Be'hay al-Koly, *Islam and the Modern Woman* (Kuwait: The Pen House, 1984), 241.

5. *Sahih Bukhari*, vol. 1, bk. 9, no. 493, narrated by 'Aisha, http://www.usc.edu/dept/MSA/fundamentals/hadithsunnah/ bukhari/009.sbt.html (accessed June 11, 2007).

6. Ibid., vol. 1, bk. 2, no. 28, narrated by Ibn 'Abbas, http:// www.usc.edu/dept/MSA/fundamentals/hadithsunnah/ bukhari/002.sbt.html (accessed June 11, 2007).

7. Imam Ghazali, *Eh'he'yat A'lum A'din*, vol. 2. He was quoting the Islamic scholar al-Shafa'a.

8. Ahmed To'fa'ha, *Women and Islam*, 180.

9. Abu Bakr Ahmad Ibn Abd Allah Ibn Mousa al-Kanadi, *Al-Musanaf*, vol. 1, pt. 2, p. 263.

10. *Sahih Bukhari*, vol. 7, bk. 62, no. 33, narrated by Usama bin Zaid, http://www.usc.edu/dept/MSA/fundamentals/ hadithsunnah/bukhari/062.sbt.html (accessed June 11, 2007).

11. Ibid., vol. 7, bk. 62, no. 113, narrated by Abu Huraira, http://www.usc.edu/dept/MSA/fundamentals/hadithsunnah/ bukhari/062.sbt.html (accessed June 11, 2007).

12. Ibid., vol. 4, bk. 52, no. 110, narrated by 'Abdullah bin 'Umar, http://www.usc.edu/dept/MSA/fundamentals/ hadithsunnah/bukhari/052.sbt.html (accessed June 11, 2007).

10 — Islamic Law About Marriage

1. See *Sahih Bukhari*, vol. 7, bk. 62, no. 88, narrated by 'Ursa, http://www.usc.edu/dept/MSA/fundamentals/hadithsunnah/bukhari/062.sbt.html (accessed June 11, 2007).

2. See *Sahih Muslim*, bk. 9, nos. 3507–3511, http://www.usc.edu/dept/MSA/fundamentals/hadithsunnah/muslim/009.smt.html (accessed June 11, 2007).

3. See Ibn Kathir, *The Beginning and the End* (Beirut, Lebanon: Revival of the Arabic Tradition Publishing House, 2001).

4. *Sahih Bukhari*, vol. 7, bk. 62, no. 142, narrated by Anas bin Malik, http://www.usc.edu/dept/MSA/fundamentals/hadithsunnah/bukhari/062.sbt.html (accessed June 11, 2007).

5. Ibn Isad, *The Great Classes*, vol. 8, p. 139.

6. Imam Ghazali, *Eh'he'yat A'lum A'din,* vol. 2, p. 27.

7. You can get an amazingly detailed picture of Muslim society by reading a few chapters from book 9 of the *Sahih Muslim*, one of the most respected collections. There you will find 104 accounts about Muhammad's conflicts with his wives, specific divorces within the community, and divorce regulations. This full chapter is available at http://www.usc.edu/dept/MSA/fundamentals/hadithsunnah/muslim/009.smt.html.

8. See *Sahih Muslim*, bk. 9, nos. 3491–3493, http://www.usc.edu/dept/MSA/fundamentals/hadithsunnah/muslim/009.smt.html (accessed June 11, 2007).

11 — Women's Rights Under Islam

1. *Sahih Bukhari*, vol. 1, bk. 6, no. 321, narrated by Aiyub, http://www.usc.edu/dept/MSA/fundamentals/hadithsunnah/bukhari/006.sbt.html (accessed June 11, 2007).

2. See Iqra Islamic Publications, "Great Muslim Women Companions of Prophet Muhammad," http://www.iqra .net/articles/muslims/great_women.php (accessed June 11, 2007); and Middle East Media Research Institute, special dispatch series, "Al-Qa'ida Women's Magazine: Women Must Participate in Jihad," no. 779, September 7, 2004, http:// memri.org/bin/articles.cgi?Page=archives&Area=sd&ID=SP77 904 (accessed June 11, 2007).

3. I obtained this information from Dr. Qaradawi's Web site in Arabic at www.qaradawi.net.

12 — Loss of Freedom for Women

1. Muhammad Sayyid Ramadan al-Bhuti, *For Every Muslim Girl Who Believes in Allah and the Last Day* (Cairo, Egypt: Al-Azhar Student Society, 1982), 98. Dr. al-Bhuti is a professor at the Islamic university in Medina and one of the most famous scholars and writers of our modern history. His status is similar to that of Dr. Yusef Qaradawi.

2. Richard Kerbaj, "Mufti Outrages Muslims Over Sex Comments," *The Australian*, October 27, 2006, http://www .theaustralian.news.com.au/story/0,20867,20652759-601,00. html (accessed June 11, 2007).

3. Muhammad Sayyid Ramadan al-Bhuti, *For Every Muslim Girl Who Believes in Allah and the Last Day*, 43.

4. Ibid., 45

5. *Sahih Bukhari*, vol. 3, bk. 29, no. 85, narrated by Ibn 'Abbas, http://www.usc.edu/dept/MSA/fundamentals/hadithsunnah/ bukhari/029.sbt.html (accessed June 11, 2007).

6. Ibid., vol. 3, bk. 29, no. 87, narrated by Qaza'a, http://www .usc.edu/dept/MSA/fundamentals/hadithsunnah/bukhari/029. sbt.html (accessed June 11, 2007).

7. Ibid., vol. 4, bk. 52, no. 250, narrated by Ibn Abbas, http://www.usc.edu/dept/MSA/fundamentals/hadithsunnah/bukhari/052.sbt.html (accessed June 11, 2007).

8. Agence France-Presse, "Saudi Gang-Rape Victim Faces 90 Lashes" March 5, 2007, as quoted by *Kaleej Times Online*, http://www.khaleejtimes.com/DisplayArticleNew.asp?section=middleeast&xfile=data/middleeast/2007/march/middleeast_march71.xml (accessed June 11, 2007).

9. *Sahih Bukhari*, vol. 9, bk. 88, no. 219, narrated by Abu Bakra, http://www.usc.edu/dept/MSA/fundamentals/hadithsunnah/bukhari/088.sbt.html (accessed June 11, 2007).

10. Yusef Qaradawi, *A Modern Islamic Legal Opinion*, vol. 1 (Beirut, Lebanon: Oli No'ha, n.d.), 73.

13 — Seven Ways Islamic Law Clashes With Western Law

1. See *Sahih Muslim*, bk. 19, no. 4436. This story is contained in chapter 41 of *Sahih Muslim*, which is titled "The Murder of Ka'b b. Ashraf," which translates "The Evil Genius of the Jews."

2. Abdul Salam Faraj, "Deception of the Infidels Is an Art of War," in *The Abandoned Duty*, quoted in Rifaat Sayed Ahmed, *The Armed Prophet*.

3. Someone who has their own copy of the Quran may continue reading in this chapter and say, "Dr. Gabriel, the Quran says that if the apostates don't fight the Muslims, then the Muslims shouldn't fight them. So maybe verse 89 only refers to killing apostates who fight Islam." My response is that Surah 4:90 only gives a small loophole of protection. Muhammad had entered into treaties with some groups who were not Muslim. If an apostate had belonged to one of those groups before he accepted Islam, he could return to them and the Muslims would not kill him as long as he did not violate

the terms of that treaty. Here's how this principle would be applied today. Egypt and the United States have a friendly relationship, or treaty. If an Egyptian Muslim converted to Christianity and moved to America, he would be protected by the treaty between Egypt and America. But if this convert did something to violate this treaty, then Muslims would be permitted to kill him. An example of a violation would be speaking publicly about his conversion.

4. *Sahih Bukhari*, vol. 9, bk. 84, no. 57, narrated by 'Ikrima, http://www.usc.edu/dept/MSA/fundamentals/hadithsunnah/bukhari/084.sbt.html (accessed June 11, 2007).

5. *Malik's Muwatta*, bk. 41, no. 41.1.5, http://www.usc.edu/dept/MSA/fundamentals/hadithsunnah/muwatta/041.mmt.html (accessed June 11, 2007).

6. *Sahih Muslim*, bk. 17, no. 4206, http://www.usc.edu/dept/MSA/fundamentals/hadithsunnah/muslim/017.smt.html (accessed June 11, 2007).

7. Ibid., bk. 17, no. 4226, http://www.usc.edu/dept/MSA/fundamentals/hadithsunnah/muslim/017.smt.html (accessed June 11, 2007).

8. I was also taught that a Muslim's desire for food in paradise will be met in the same way. There will be many wonderful fruits, and the air will be filled with beautiful birds. If a Muslim sees a bird and desires it for food, he will find immediately that the bird comes in front of him, prepared to be eaten on a beautiful platter.

9. *Sunan an-Nisai*, vol. 4, no. 4928.

10. Ibid., vol. 4, no. 4992.

11. See Surah 24; and *Sahih Bukhari*, vol. 3, bk. 48, no. 829, narrated by 'Aisha, http://www.usc.edu/dept/MSA/fundamentals/hadithsunnah/bukhari/048.sbt.html (accessed June 11, 2007).

12. Ibn Kathir, *The Quran Commentary*, vol. 3, pt. 6, p. 21–22.

13. Ibid., vol. 1, p. 273.

14. Ibid.

14 — What Islam Teaches About Democracy

1. Condoleezza Rice, "Remarks at the American University in
    Cairo," June 20, 2005, as quoted at U.S. Department of State,
    http://www.state.gov/secretary/rm/2005/48328.htm (accessed
    June 11, 2007).

    In the same speech, Rice wisely acknowledged the
    shortcoming of the United States in human rights: "In my
    own country, the progress of democracy has been long and
    difficult. And given our history, the United States has no
    cause for false pride and we have every reason for humility.

    "After all, America was founded by individuals who knew
    that all human beings—and the governments they create—
    are inherently imperfect. And the United States was born half
    free and half slave. And it was only in my lifetime that my
    government guaranteed the right to vote for all of its people.

    "Nevertheless, the principles enshrined in our Constitution
    enable citizens of conviction to move America closer every
    day to the ideal of democracy. Here in the Middle East,
    that same long hopeful process of democratic change is now
    beginning to unfold. Millions of people are demanding
    freedom for themselves and democracy for their countries."

2. WashingtonPost.com, "Full Text of Iraqi Constitution: Draft
    Document, to Be Presented to Voters Saturday," courtesy of
    the Associated Press, October 12, 2005, http://www
    .washingtonpost.com/wp-dyn/content/article/2005/10/12/
    AR2005101201450.html (accessed June 11, 2007).

3. Arab Republic of Egypt, The People's Assembly, "Constitution
    Text," http://www.parliament.gov.eg/EPA/en/itemX.jsp
    ?itemFlag="Strange"&categoryID=1&sectionID=11&

typeID=1&categoryIDX=1&itemID=8&levelid=54&
parentlevel=6&levelno=2 (accessed June 11, 2007).

4. The following is a sample of the most prominent Islamic
   scholars who have rejected democracy and demand Islamic
   government. I read these books in Arabic, but you can find
   English translations for some of them, especially the books
   by Maududi and Qutb: Syed Abu-ala' Maududi, *Theory of
   Islam and Its Guidance*, 33–34; Sayyid Qutb, *Milestones
   Along the Road*, 81; Abdul Hamid Mut'wa'li, *The Principle
   of Shura*, 40; Mohamed As'sad, *Islam and Politics*, 52;
   Ta'kay al-Neb'han'i, *The Islamic Personality*, vol. 3, p. 9; and
   Mahmoud al-Kah'li'di, *Western Democracy in the Light of
   the Islamic Law*.

5. Mahmoud al-Kah'lidi, *Western Democracy in the Light of
   Islamic Law*. I knew Dr. al-Kah'lidi when he was studying
   for his doctorate in Islamic law at Al-Azhar in the 1980s.

6. Syed Abu-ala' Maududi, *The Islamic State*.

7. The following is a sample of the most prominent Islamic
   scholars who accept democracy. I read these books in Arabic,
   and you will probably have a hard time finding any in
   English, with the possible exception of the books by Sheikh
   Yusef Qaradawi: Yusef Qaradawi, *A Modern Islamic Legal
   Opinion*; Dayima al-Jourff, *Theory of the State*, 371–373;
   Abdullah al-Arabi, *A Discussion of the Constitution*, 224;
   Muhammad Be'Keet al-Mute'e, *The Truth of Islam and
   the Principle of the Government,* 24; Mohamed al-Ri'yes,
   Political Theory, 338; Shi'keeb Ar-Salan, *The Islamic World
   Today*, vol. 1, p. 240; Mustafa Sabri, *The Relationship
   Between Mind, and Science, and the World*, vol. 1, p. 18;
   Abas al-A'kaad, *Democracy in Islam*, 54; and Sayyid Sa'biq,
   The Element of the Power in Islam, 199. Sheikh Sa'biq was

the imam of the mosque in Cairo where I said my prayers while earning my bachelor's degree at Al-Azhar. Almost every Friday, I would sit and discuss issues with him because he was an Al-Azhar scholar. He has already died.

8. Yusef Qaradawi, *A Modern Islamic Legal Opinion,* vol. 2, p. 636–652.

9. *Sahih Muslim,* bk. 20, no. 4574, http://www.usc.edu/dept/ MSA/fundamentals/hadithsunnah/muslim/020.smt.html (accessed June 11, 2007).

10. Yusef Qaradawi, *A Modern Islamic Legal Opinion,* vol. 2, p. 636–652.

11. Ibid.

15 — Establishing Democracy in Iraq and the Middle East

1. Charles Levinson, "$50 Billion Later, Taking Stock of U.S. Aid to Egypt," *Christian Science Monitor,* April 12, 2004, http://www.csmonitor.com/2004/0412/p07s01-wome.html (accessed June 11, 2007).

16 — Separating Religion and Politics

1. The Constitution of the Islamic Republic of Iran, article 1. The full English translation is available at http://www .iranonline.com/Iranhall/index-IOL.html (accessed June 11, 2007).

2. Ibid., article 64.

3. Ibid., article 74.

4. Ibid., article 91.

5. Ibid., article 2.

6. Ibid., article 94.

17 — Fifty Years From Now

1. This is my personal estimate based on my understanding of the Quran. It was also previously published in my book *Islam and Terrorism* (Lake Mary, FL: Charisma House, 2002).

18 — The War of Ideas

1. International Freedom of Expression Exchange, "Spain: Supreme Court Upholds Conviction of Al-Jazeera Journalist," http://www.ifex.org/en/content/view/full/74905/ (accessed June 11, 2007).

Glossary

THE GLOSSARY INCLUDES AN INFORMAL PRONUNCIATION guide for words that are difficult to pronounce. The pronunciation guides are intended to improve ease of reading and do not reflect formal linguistic standards for phonetic spellings.

AH   Means "after *hijra*." The Islamic calendar starts in the year that Muhammad made the *hijra* from Mecca to Medina.

amah   Female slave

amir   Leader or commander

apostate   One who renounces his religion

apostasy, laws of   Islamic law regarding the treatment of an apostate from Islam

Al-Azhar   The oldest, largest, and most powerful Islamic university in the world, based in Cairo, Egypt.

Bakr, Abu [*AW-bu BAW-kir*]   Close companion of Muhammad and first caliph after Muhammad's death

Banna, Hasan al- (1906–1949)   Founder of the Muslim Brotherhood, the grandfather of all modern Muslim radical groups

caliph   An Arabic word that means "leader." The term *caliph* specifically refers to the successors of Muhammad who served as the political and spiritual heads of Islam.

caliphate   The office or dominion of the caliph. The last caliphate was based in Turkey until its fall in 1924.

dhu-mahram A woman's husband or a man that she cannot marry according to Islamic law, such as her brother or father-in-law. Islamic law says that a woman must be accompanied by a duh-mahram when she travels.

hadith *[ha-DEETH]* The record of Muhammad's words and actions. This material was committed to memory for several generations and then collected and recorded by Muslim scholars. The most reliable collections were put together by al-Bukhari (ah 194–256) and Muslim (ah 202–261).

hajj A pilgrimage to Mecca performed by observant Muslims at least once during a lifetime if possible.

ijma'ah *[EEJ-muh-yuh]* Means "a group in agreement." It refers to the practice in Islamic law whereby new law is established for situations not specifically covered in the Quran or sunnah.

infidel Anyone who does not accept the message of Islam

Islam The religion founded by Muhammad. Its beliefs are based on the Quran and the life of Muhammad. Followers of Islam are called Muslims.

Islamic world The countries where most people practice Islam. There are about fifty-five Islamic countries in the world.

kafir An infidel, meaning someone who does not accept the message of Islam

Khattib, Umar ibn al- Second successor of Muhammad.

Maududi, Syed Abu-ala' (1903–1979) *[AW-bool ah-la-mow-DOO-dee]* Maududi's prolific writing focused on reviving fundamentalist Islam, and he was instrumental in the creation of Pakistan with the intention of making it a Muslim state. His writings are widely available in Arabic,

English, and other languages.

Muslim A person who practices Islam.

nasikh The principle of continuing revelation in the Quran. In the case of a contradiction, newer teachings abrogate, or cancel, older teachings.

Nasser, Gemal Abdul President of Egypt from 1956–1970

People of the Book The phrase used in the Quran and hadith to refer to Jews and Christians because they received holy books from God

Ottoman Empire Muslim caliphate lasting from 1301–1924

Quran The compilation of the revelations Muhammad received from the angel Gabriel. The Quran is 114 surahs (chapters) long, which is about the length of the New Testament.

Qutb, Sayyid (1906–1965) *[SAH-yeed KOO-tib; OO as in foot]* Of all radical writings, Sayyid Qutb's are the most widely read and circulated, particularly his book Milestones Along the Road, for which he was executed by the Egyptian government in 1965.

raka'ah A unit of prayer according to Islamic teaching. A Muslim will perform two or more raka'ahs at each of the five daily prayer times.

Ramadan Islamic holy month during which Muslims fast from food and liquids between the first and fourth prayers of the day

sharia *[SHAH-ree-uh]* Islamic law based first on the Quran (revelation from Allah), then on sunnah (example of Muhammad), and finally on *ijma'ah* (the informed decision of a qualified group of Muslim scholars).

al-shurra To make decisions by consulting together

Sufism Islamic sect that was most popular during the time of Ibn Taymiyyah. It focuses on the inner, personal life of Muslims and rejects jihad as a physical battle in favor of jihad as a battle within oneself to follow the teachings of Islam.

sunnah The words and actions of Muhammad, the prophet of Islam. The record of these words and actions is called hadith.

surah Chapter

Taymiyyah, Ibn (1268–1328) *[ib-in tie-MEE-yuh]* A conservative Islamic scholar who is often quoted by radicals

Umayyad Dynasty Muslim caliphate lasting from AH 41–132 / AD 661–751.

usury Charging interest for a loan

Bibliography

Ahmed, Rifaat Sayed. *The Armed Prophet*. London: Riad El-Rayyes Books, 1991. In Arabic.

al-, Muhammad Sayyid Ramadan, *For Every Muslim Girl Who Believes in Allah and the Last Day*. Cairo, Egypt: Al-Azhar Student Society, 1982. In Arabic.

al-Koly, Al-Be'hay. *Islam and the Modern Woman*. Kuwait: Pen House, 1984. In Arabic.

Faraj, Abdul Salam. *The Abandoned Duty. Translated by* Habib Srouji. In Rifaat Sayed Ahmed. *The Armed Prophet*. London: Riad El-Rayyes Books, 1991.

Kathir, Ibn. *The Beginning and the End*. Beirut, Lebanon: Revival of the Arabic Tradition Publishing House, 2001. In Arabic.

———. *The Quran Commentary*. Mansura, Egypt: Faith Library, 1996. In Arabic.

Malik's Muwatta. Translated by 'A'isha 'Abdarahman at-Tarjumana and Ya'qub Johnson. Available through the USC-MSA Compendium of Muslim Texts, http://www.usc.edu/dept/MSA/fundamentals/hadithsunnah/muwatta/.

Qaradawi, Yusef. *A Modern Islamic Legal Opinion*. Beirut, Lebanon: Oli No'ha, n.d. In Arabic.

Qutb, Sayyid. *Milestones Along the Road*. Delhi, India: Markazi Maktaba Islami.

Sahih Bukhari. Translated by M. Muhsin Khan. Available through the USC-MSA Compendium of Muslim Texts, http://www.usc.edu/dept/MSA/fundamentals/hadithsunnah/bukhari/.

Sahih Muslim. Translated by Abdul Hamid Siddiqui. Available through the USC-MSA Compendium of Muslim Texts, http://www.usc.edu/dept/MSA/fundamentals/hadithsunnah/muslim/.

To'fa'ha, Ahmed. *Women and Islam*. Beirut, Lebanon: 1985

Index of Quranic References

2:47   45
2:65   67
2:120   13, 145
2:120–121   47
2:135   47
2:173   6, 34
2:178   114, 134, 135
2:183–185   27
2:187   28, 29
2:189   34
2:196   29
2:219   114, 127
2:221   54, 58
2:223   90
2:228   92
2:231   93
2:236   93
2:241   93
2:276   37
2:278–279   37
2:282   39, 80, 81
3:28   55
3:64   67
3:73   46
3:85   12, 120
3:90–91   121
3:97   29
3:110   45, 64, 65
3:118   46
3:151   156
3:159   147
4:29   155
4:34   77, 85, 89
4:43   35
4:64   138
4:65   137, 144
4:80   138

4:86   36
4:88–89   113
4:89   119
4:101   23
4:102   23
4:103   24
4:105   144, 149
4:124   96
4:144   55
4:150   137
4:150–151   103
4:176   81
5:5   57, 58
5:6   20, 22
5:33   113, 115, 119
5:38   114, 130
5:44   138
5:47   144
5:49–50   138
5:51   48, 55
5:56   56
5:57   56
5:60   67
5:72–73   53
5:78   45, 54
5:80   56
5:82   13, 48
5:90   35
5:90–91   114, 127
5:97   29
5:101   4, 133
7:3   144
7:33   143
7:54   143
7:166   67
8:12   156
8:60   156
9:23   52, 54

9:28   44
9:71   99
9:123   69
12:40   143
16:58–59   69, 76
16:106   120
16:116   144
17:111   143
18:26   143
18:28   145
22:27   30
24:2   113, 124
24:4   131, 133
24:4–5   133
24:11–20   132
24:13   114, 132
24:31   102
24:51   4
24:55   149
25:77   120
28:38   148
29:46   67
30:21   88
33:4   41
33:59   101
38:26   138
42:11–18   87
42:38   146
46:15   85
48:29   69
52:20   90
58:22   51
59:7   4, 133
65:2   91
65:4   91
65:6   92
76:5, 15, 19   129
81:8–9   76

Index

A

Abraham 30–31, 47
Abraham's grave 30–31
abrogation 35
Abu Ghraib *xiv*
adoption *x*, 33, 39–42
adultery 7, 87, 113, 121,
   123–127, 131–132
Aisha 81, 86–87, 130, 132
alcohol 33–35, 62, 114,
   127–129
Ali, Ayaan Hirsi *x*
amah 87, 190
amir 115, 118, 190
apostasy 6, 113, 119, 121–123,
   190
Arabiyya, Al- 172
Ashraf, Ka'ab ibn al- 116
Assad, Hafex al- 66
Assmah, al- 115–116
Azhar University, Al- *viii, xii,
   xvi,* 59–60, 106, 129, 142,
   190

B

Baghdad 152–154
Bakr, Abu 63, 66, 106, 111,
   128, 190
Bana, Hassan al- 142
beating wives *xi*, 89
Bedouin 2, 5, 65, 68–69, 84
Black Stone 5, 30

Book, the 45, 47, 56, 58, 64
Buddhism 122
Buddhist(s) 44, 57–58,
   122–123

C

caliph 10, 30, 66, 125, 190
caliphate 128, 154, 190,
   192–193
cartoon controversy 117
Christian(s) 12–14, 33, 40–41,
   44–45, 47–48, 52–55,
   57–58, 64–65, 67, 76,
   121–122, 126, 135, 145,
   154, 158, 162, 164, 192
Christianity *x,* 5, 13–14, 51,
   122, 126, 145, 153
committed Muslim *x–xv,* 19,
   24, 33, 53, 83, 95, 97–98,
   103
cruel and unusual punishment
   113–114, 123, 127, 129,
   131, 134
Crusades 12, 14

D

democracy 65, 138–151,
   154–155, 157–161
dhu-mahram 104
divorce *x,* 41, 88–94, 103

E

Egypt *viii, xi–xv,* 2, 7, 54, 60–61, 65–66, 77, 96, 100, 106, 111, 123, 135–136, 141, 157–160, 174, 190, 192

F

fajr, al- 7–8
fasting *x,* 3, 7, 17, 21, 24–28
Fedat, Abdul 98
female slave (see *amah*) 87–88, 190
first amendment 113, 118, 123
followers of the Book 45, 64
Friday sermons 117

G

Great Britain 154
Guantanamo Bay *xiv*

H

hadith *viii, xii,* 14, 19, 36–37, 83–84, 86, 89–90, 93, 102, 104, 106, 112, 119, 125, 128, 147, 150, 169, 175–176, 191–193
hajj 5, 29–31, 104, 191
Hanbal 103
Harith, Juwaryriya bint al- 87
hell 11, 27, 54, 103, 120
hijab x, xii, xiv, 103
Hindu(s) 44, 57–58
Hizb-at-Dawa 152–153
Ho-yay, Safiya bint 87
honor killing 121, 135–136

Hussein, Saddam 63, 66, 70, 139, 152–153, 172

I

idol worshipers 5–6, 36, 53, 57–58, 65, 132
ijma'ah 112, 191, 192
imam *viii, x,* 7, 10–11, 21, 27, 54, 85, 101, 170
infidel 11, 43, 70, 135, 142, 145, 147, 154–156, 191
interest charged for a loan 33, 37–38, 193
intoxicants (see alcohol) 35, 114, 127
Iran *xi, xiii, xv,* 2, 63, 106, 151–152, 154, 157, 159, 161–162, 167
Iraq *xiv–xv,* 2, 30, 39, 63, 66, 138–139, 141, 151–158, 160, 172
Ishmael 30
Islamic law (see sharia) *xii–xv,* 18–19, 39–40, 75, 87–88, 91, 93–94, 102–104, 106, 108, 111–112, 115, 117–119, 121, 123, 127–131, 135, 137, 140–141, 143, 145, 149–150, 156, 162, 168, 170, 175, 190–192
Israel *ix,* 12–13, 45, 51, 53–54, 63, 168

J

Jazeera, Al- 147, 170, 172–173

Jerusalem 154

Jew(s) 6, 12–14, 41, 44–45, 47–48, 53, 55, 57–58, 64, 67, 121, 132, 135, 145, 162, 192

Jewish 4, 6, 13–14, 46, 57–58, 65, 67–68, 76, 87, 116

jihad *x, xii–xiii, xv,* 82, 96–99, 147, 169, 175–176, 193

Jordan 135, 154

Judaism 12–13, 51

K

Ka'aba, Al- 6, 30–31, 45

kafir 43, 145, 191

Khadija 86–87

Khattib, Umar ibn al- 10, 83, 191

khula, al- 94

Kurd(s) 151–153, 155

Kurdish 152

L

Laden, Osama bin *xi,* 173

liberal Muslims *ix, xiv,* 141, 170, 175–176

Libya 66, 68, 157–160

M

major wash (see washing) 19, 20–22

marriage 21, 58, 75, 86–89, 93

Maslama, Muhammad ibn 116

Maududi, Syed Abu-ala' 142–143, 191

Mecca 2, 5, 29–31, 34, 36, 44–45, 65, 75–76, 96, 104, 190–191

media *xiii–xv,* 11–12, 17, 75, 117–118, 169, 171–174

Medina 2, 23, 31–32, 34, 36, 57, 65, 81, 87, 104, 111, 153, 190

Middle East *vii, xi–xii, xiv,* 13, 26, 63, 75, 83–84, 100, 118, 122, 138–139, 151, 154, 157–158, 160, 164, 172

minor wash (see washing) 19–22

mosque(s) *viii, x, xii, xvi,* 7, 9–10, 18, 21–22, 29, 31, 44–45, 54, 100–102

Muawiyya 63, 66

Muhammad *vii–viii, xi–xiii, xv–xvi,* 1–7, 9–12, 14, 18–19, 21–23, 25–42, 44, 47, 50–51, 57, 65–66, 68–70, 75–88, 90–91, 96–97, 100, 104, 106, 111–112, 115–117, 119, 121, 124–126, 130–133, 135, 137–138, 144, 146–148, 156, 169, 172, 174, 176, 190–193

mujadin 173

murder *xii,* 69, 114, 116, 134–135, 137, 141

Muslim World League *xv*

N

najasun 44
nasikh 35, 192
Nasser, Gamal Abdel 66, 192
New Testament 192

O

Old Testament 6
ordinary, secular Muslim(s)
    ix–x
Ottoman Empire 59, 192

P

paradise 3, 85, 90, 96, 128–129
people of the Book 45, 56, 58,
    192
pilgrimage (see *hajj*) 5, 17,
    24–25, 29–30, 34, 37, 96,
    191
poet(s) 116, 133
poetry 10, 115–116, 132
prayer *x*, 3, 6–9, 17–26, 28–29,
    31, 33–35, 37, 68, 79, 81,
    90, 99–100, 127, 148, 192

Q

Qaddafi, Muammar al- 66,
    158–160
Qaeda, Al- *xi*, 98, 153, 168,
    173
Qaradawi, Yusef 98–99,
    106–107, 147–149, 170
Quran *viii–xvi*, 1, 4–5, 7, 11,
    13–14, 21, 23–24, 29, 31,
    34–35, 37–38, 42–48,
50–54, 57–58, 62–63, 66,
    68, 76–78, 81, 85, 87–91,
    101–103, 107, 112–115,
    119–120, 124–125,
    127–133, 137–138, 140,
    142–150, 155–156, 161–
    162, 169–170, 175–176,
    191–192
Qutb, Sayyid 60, 142, 192

R

radical Muslim(s) *xiii–xv*, 9, 97,
    99, 137, 141, 173
raka'ah 3, 7–8, 18–19, 31, 81,
    192
Ramadan *ix*, *xii*, 3, 20, 25–29,
    34, 96, 101, 103, 192
rape 101, 105–106
rebellion 46, 103, 113, 115,
    118
Rice, Condoleeza 139

S

Sadat, Anwar 141
Saudi Arabia 5, 45, 88, 105,
    130, 154, 172
secular Muslim(s) (see ordinary,
    secular Muslims) *x*
sex 20–22, 69, 88, 90, 113,
    123–124
shame 69, 75–76, 106, 121
sharia 111–112, 118, 127–128,
    134–135, 141, 192
Shia 63, 152

Shiite(s) 19, 66, 151–153,
    155–157
shurra, al- 146, 193
slander *xii*, 114, 131–133
sobh, al- 7
stealing *xii*, 114, 129–131, 143
stereotyping *xv*, 17, 43–44, 48,
    75, 77–78, 94, 176
stoning 113, 125–127
Sufism 193
suicide bomb 98–99
sunnah 7, 130, 191–193
Sunni(s) 18, 63, 66, 98, 106,
    117, 151–153, 155–157
Syria *xiv*, 2, 63, 65–66, 152,
    154

T

Turkey 2, 152, 154, 190

U

United States *xi*, 2, 107, 114,
    118, 122–123, 129, 134,
    139, 155, 157–161, 164,
    173
usury (see interest) 37–38, 193

V

veils 102

W

washing 7, 17–24
West, the *vii*, *x–xii*, *xiv–xvi*, 2,
    43, 59–60, 108, 111, 117,
    142, 146, 158–159, 169,
    172–175
Western *vii*, *ix*, *xiv*, 52, 59,
    111, 117, 141–142, 154,
    171, 173
wives of Muhammad 41,
    81–82, 86–90, 132
women, rights *x*, *xii*, *xiv*, 17–
    18, 21–22, 27–28, 38, 53,
    57–58, 68, 75–87, 89–107,
    116, 127, 131, 133, 150

Z

Zaid 40–42
Zaineb 40–42

Author's Academic Credentials

Mark Gabriel's academic credentials in Islamic scholarship include:

- Bachelor's, master's, and doctorate degrees in Islamic history and culture from Al-Azhar University, Cairo, Egypt
- Graduating second in his class of six thousand students for his bachelor's degree. This ranking was based on cumulative scores of oral and written exams given at the end of each school year.
- Being one of the youngest lecturers ever hired at Al-Azhar University. He started lecturing after he finished his master's degree and while working to finish his doctorate.
- Traveling lecturer. The university sent him to countries around the Middle East as a lecturer in Islamic history.

Al-Azhar University is the most respected, authoritative Islamic university in the world. It has been in continuous operation for more than one thousand years.

In addition to his academic training, Dr. Gabriel had practical experience serving as the imam at a mosque in the Cairo suburbs.

After Dr. Gabriel became a Christian in 1993, he pursued a Christian education. His credentials in Christian education include:

- Discipleship training school with Youth With a Mission in Cape Town, South Africa (1996)
- Master's degree in world religion from Florida Christian University in Orlando, Florida (2001)
- Doctorate degree in Christian education from Florida
Christian University in Orlando, Florida (2002)
- Induction as a fellow in the Oxford Society of Scholars (2003)

Dr. Gabriel is president and founder of Union of Former Muslims (www.unionofformermuslims.com).

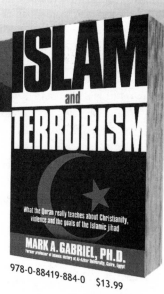